MARRIED TO A MARTYR

A story of tragedy and hope

MARRIED TO A MARTYR

A story of tragedy and hope

The authorised biography of Susanne Geske

Jonathan Carswell and Joanna Wright

Authentic

MILTON KEYNES ● COLORADO SPRINGS ● HYDERABAD

British Library Cataloguing in Publication Data
A catalogue record for this book is available from the British Library
ISBN-13: 978-1-85078-816

Unless otherwise stated, Scripture quotations are taken from the HOLY BIBLE, NEW
INTERNATIONAL VERSION. Copyright © 1973, 1978, 1984 by the International Bible
Society. Used by permission of Hodder & Stoughton Limited. All rights reserved. 'NIV'
is a registered trademark of the International Bible Society UK trademark number
1448790; and THE MESSAGE. Copyright © 1993, 1994, 1995, 1996, 2000, 2001, 2002.
Used by permission of NavPress Publishing Group
Please note that where mission organizations are referred to in the text, they are not
identified by name. This is to protect the safety of their workers and the future of their
work. Excerpts from 'Blessed be Your Name' by Beth and Matt Redman Copyright ©
2002 Thankyou Music. Used with permission; 'Father God, I Wonder' by Ian Smale.
Copyright © 1984 Ian Smale, Thankyou Music. Used with permission. Administered
by worshiptogether.com songs excluding UK & Europe and by kingswaysongs.com,
tym@kingsway.co.uk; 'How Can I Keep from Singing?' © 2006 Alletrop Music/BMI
(administered by Music Services)/Worshiptogether.com Songs/Sixsteps Music
ASCAP/ThankYou Music (administered by EMI Christian Music Publishing). All
Rights Reserved. Used by Permission.

Cover design by James Kessell for Scratch the Sky Ltd.
(www.scratchthesky.com)
Print Management by Adare
Printed and bound in Great Britain by J.H. Haynes & Co., Sparkford

To William MacDonald

Though I never met him, his writings in *True Discipleship* have had a profound effect on my Christian life. I describe reading it as 'sitting on a spiritual cactus – it leaves you feeling uncomfortable'. I believe it is the single most important book apart from the Bible for Christians to read. Even if only half the book's message is taken on board, it will change your walk with God. It changed mine and therefore I, with a sincere heart, want to thank the late William MacDonald.

JDC

Contents

Acknowledgements

This work was by far the biggest undertaking of our lives so far. We wish to thank Susanne for inviting us into her life and home while she was still grieving. Her honesty and generosity were overwhelming. We admire and commend her dedication to those to whom she has been called to minister.

While away in Turkey writing and researching, many of our family (church family and natural family) were praying for us. We were humbled by your love and support.

Thank you to Anna who assisted us with our translation and Mark who gave us this opportunity. Charlotte, our editor, worked with great skill and patience – thank you.

We have great admiration for those who, day in, day out, stand up and speak out for the persecuted church. They are heroes – thank you for what you do. May the worldwide church wake up to the need to help our brothers and sisters who face maltreatment of all kinds.

Jonathan Carswell
Joanna Wright
Northern Ireland, 2008

Introduction

It was Wednesday afternoon and already rumours were circulating around the world. Whisperings and mutterings via email and phone were spreading news of a terrible, triple murder – but nothing was yet confirmed. Without a doubt, something horrific had happened but reports were sketchy at best, frequently embellished and exaggerated.

As hearsay was replaced with hard evidence, it was clear that Susanne Geske had become a martyr's widow, far from home, in Malatya, eastern Turkey.

We were given exclusive access to the story of this extraordinarily resolute woman in whom, until 18 April 2007, the world had no interest. With so many aggrandized stories being told as fact, we sought the truth from the one person who could provide it with complete authority.

This is the remarkable story of Susanne Geske . . .

For the safety of those still working in the field, the names and some place names in this book have been changed, except those of Susanne and her family.

'If you confess your sins and believe in Jesus . . .'

The alarm clock sounded particularly unforgiving as the early morning sunlight broke through a gap in the curtains. With heavy eyes, Susanne rolled over, her arm falling onto her husband's pillow. She felt nothing. Waking gradually, she moved her hand down expecting to find Tilmann. He wasn't there: she found nothing. In her dazed state she realized this was not a dream. Tilmann was gone: gone forever.

Life for Susanne Beuter wasn't easy. Her parents had divorced when she was just five years old and custody of her and her siblings was split between them. Her parents found it hard to cope and Susanne spent some time with foster parents. Susanne's mother refused to allow her to go to them permanently, as she would not give her up completely. Life was unsettled. Like many children of divorced parents, Susanne was unsure to whom she belonged.

Finally, at the age of twenty, she was able to gain some independence and move to her own place. It is hard to convey how much this meant to her.

Christianity wasn't even considered in her parents' lives and so when Susanne moved to Beuren, Germany, to study, religion was not on the agenda. She was there to take her apprenticeship in pottery, something she loved. While it was not the most glamorous adventure a twenty-one year old could take, Susanne was no bore. She was feisty enough to hold her own, quite happily wearing provocative clothing to get attention. She was a popular girl and had a good group of friends.

One normal day, after spending hours at the wheel, Susanne heard a knock at the door. When she opened it there stood a complete stranger, casually dressed. He looked ordinary, and Susanne thought he was here to sell her something. To some extent he was . . . he introduced himself as a Christian pastor from the local church. Baffled, Susanne listened to what he had to say. She certainly didn't think a pastor would wear such trendy, 'normal' clothes.

'I heard you're a Protestant,' he said, 'and you have just moved here, right?'

The longer this stranger stood in front of Susanne the more perplexed she became. 'Firstly,' she thought, 'how on earth does this guy, whom I have never met before, know I have just moved here – has he been stalking me or something? OK, maybe he has just seen me around the village. There are after all only about six hundred people living here. A new face will stick out like a sore thumb. But secondly and more importantly, how does he know I am a Protestant and not a Catholic? This chap is scary!'

Although she did it herself, to call Susanne a Protestant was to be generous. Yes, she wasn't a Catholic, but she was more 'neutral' than Protestant. She hadn't been to church in years and there was certainly nothing in her life that would even vaguely count as religious.

The man kept talking. To both his and her surprise Susanne kept listening. 'Would you like to come to church? We'd love to see you there.'

It was a simple recruitment call but for some reason it worked. Partly out of politeness and partly out of genuine interest, Susanne responded. 'So when does it start and where do you meet?'

Smiling, the pastor answered. However it was not a satisfactory reply, from Susanne's point of view. First, the church met 25 kilometres away. If this wasn't enough to put her off, the 10 a.m. service start surely was. There was no way she was going to get up at that time of the morning, travel across country, all in aid of going to church. She might claim to be a Protestant by default but that didn't call for early treks to a church service.

'We'll see,' Susanne replied.

The pastor had heard this before and knew what it meant. He wasn't stupid! No doubt he foresaw the improbability of Susanne's attendance as soon as he mentioned the time it started. 'OK, so a 10 a.m. service 25 kilometres away might not suit, but once a month we have a service down the road, a couple of villages away, in the Catholic church – why don't you come to that? It's just once a month, and not too far.'

He was not going to let up. His persistence paid off.

'Right. So, once a month . . .'

Like being sold something by a door-to-door salesman, Susanne was slowly being persuaded that this was something she should do. Reluctant but intrigued, she agreed to attend the following month.

Susanne recalls her big event, 'There were five other people besides myself in a huge Catholic church; three of them were kids having their confirmation. What was I doing here? When the speaker came to speak to us, he told us we needed to read the Bible. If we did, God would speak to us personally through it. 'Hmmm, this is interesting,' I thought, 'if God is going to speak to me, I think I'll give this a try.' So I started reading my Bible in its old German writing. I was really good. I read all the way to the third book of the Bible, Leviticus. Unfortunately, I found it so boring and nothing or no one spoke to me. I thought that I must have something deeply wrong and forgot about it.'

The German Bible, with its out-of-date language and old type, was put to one side and allowed to gather dust.

❀   ❀   ❀   ❀

A couple of months later, after completing her apprenticeship, Susanne began looking for a job. She had been keen to work as a joiner, but that was seen as a man's job and so her thoughts were redirected towards pottery.

With no real prospects at home she started to look further afield. Switzerland provided the opening she needed – a job that paid money with the added bonus of being some distance away. Before long Susanne was packing her bags once more.

While she loved the beauty of Switzerland it wasn't enough. She needed company; friends. She was ready to have some fun.

In the pottery with her worked Elisabeth, a girl of a similar age.

'Hey Elisabeth, any suggestion of where I can meet some people? Our age, I mean. Do you know any good pubs or clubs?'

Elisabeth looked at her bleakly. 'I'm not so good at those things; I don't go to them that often. I know a youth group in church though.'

This was not the reply Susanne was hoping for. Church wasn't a hive of activity, or an ideal place for meeting twenty-somethings with a zest for life.

Then, the dreaded question. 'Do you want to come to the Friday evening group with me?' Not surprisingly, Susanne wasn't keen, but she had set herself up for this one. She couldn't say no. She was keen to meet new people and she might meet someone decent . . . maybe.

Getting ready to go she picked out the best outfit and made her way to the church.

'I actually enjoyed that,' she thought later that evening, 'I actually really enjoyed that!' Surprised was an understatement. She never thought being part of a church group could be such good fun.

Sunday soon came around and Elisabeth asked Susanne if she fancied coming along with her to church.

By this stage her need for friends was being exchanged for a greater intrigue regarding the message of Jesus and the fuss these people made about Him. Susanne agreed (despite the 10 a.m. start) and the two of them met outside the church, went in and sat down together.

❀   ❀   ❀   ❀

As she left church that morning, she was handed a book called *Jesus: Our Destiny*. It was written by Wilhelm Busch, a German Christian. Based on a compilation of speeches he gave on the radio, the book explores the centrality of Jesus to Christian doctrine, using stories of real people. It was easy to read, putting forward a simple yet tight case for the life-changing work of Jesus. He sought to convince those who doubt Christianity that it is indeed reasonable and that a faith in Jesus Christ is needed by every human, leading to a changed life.

'I really enjoyed the stories but they all finished in the same way "Jesus died for you . . . if you confess your sins and believe in Jesus you will be saved." How boring, I thought. Why do they all finish the same way? It's so unoriginal. This is not for me.'

With that Susanne closed the book. She was a girl with spice. She wanted originality. Conforming to the ways of a particular religion was not her idea of life.

Try as she might, however, she couldn't escape the sentence repeated at the end of each of those stories, even weeks later. Feeling guilty for yet another sin that was rearing its ugly head in her life the sentence she had read a few weeks earlier buzzed around in her head . . . *if you confess your sins and believe in Jesus . . .*

Susanne started to become aware of all the things she did wrong. She was desperate to rid herself of the sin that stuck to her, like an insect stuck to fly tape. Struggle as she might, she couldn't untangle herself from its grip on her life.

'It was the first time in my life, I think, that I realized I was a sinner without hope. I felt so convicted; so guilty; and so alone in it. Who could I talk to about my sin? I didn't want to tell anyone what I was really like – how humiliating. It was then that I acknowledged I was in a mess. For someone who likes to be in control and in charge, this was a big thing. I had cut myself off from God. Only I was to blame. My sin was like a roadblock – a big No Entry sign. It needed to be dealt with.'

In desperation, Susanne picked up the book she had been given and read the next chapter. It finished with the same monotonous challenge . . . *if you confess your sins and believe in Jesus . . .* With a sigh of defeat, Susanne placed the book to one side. 'If this is what it takes, then this is what I have to do. I have no choice. It might seem to be verging on the ritualistic, but I have to tell God what I've done. Who knows what will happen, but I have to tell Him. If it's so easy to talk to God then I will give it a try.'

As the moonlight began to stream its brilliant white light through the thin curtains Susanne began to pray.

'I prayed something very simple. I talked like God was there in the room with me, and it was fun. I actually enjoyed it! But nothing happened. Nothing changed. Just that same sentence running through my mind, going round and round like a toy train on a train track . . . or so I thought . . .'

Everything

The next day Susanne went to work as usual. Unknown to her, she bounced in with an unusual lightness in her step and a smile on her face.

'What has happened to you?!' Elisabeth asked immediately.

'Nothing.'

'Well, something has happened to you, you're different. What is it?'

'Why should I be different?'

'Tell me what has happened. You're different,' she repeated. 'What have you done?'

It dawned on Susanne that her new appearance might relate to last night. She explained to Elisabeth what had happened and how she had tried to talk to God.

Elisabeth squealed with delight and jumped up to hug her, squeezing her so tight she nearly picked her up off the ground. She was thrilled about the enormity of what Susanne had done.

Susanne tried to describe how she felt, explaining her uncertainty that anyone or anything had heard her cries that evening. For Elisabeth, there was no question however that her prayers had not just been heard but answered by Almighty God. He had miraculously transformed Susanne even if she wasn't fully aware of it.

'"How did you know something was different?" I asked. "Oh, I just knew," Elisabeth replied. "I could see it; I could see it so clearly." And that is how my life in Christ started. It was quite funny really!'

One night Susanne found herself alone in her room. Life had dramatically changed since the night she had first tried talking with God. He *had* heard her and what is more, He had supernaturally answered. She was a new person, with a new drive for life: but a life lived for God.

'I was sat on my bed that evening,' Susanne recalls, 'the place where I had cried out to God just a little while before. All my earthly possessions were laid out in front of me. There wasn't much, but it was what I had. I bowed my head once again and I remember telling the Lord that He could have all that I had. I wanted Him to have *everything*. What I had now was His; what I would have in the future was His too.'

Susanne had been a Christian barely any time, but already she knew the call of God upon her life. As Elijah said in 1 Kings 18 to the prophets of Baal, 'How long will you waver between two opinions? If the LORD is God, follow him.' No longer was Susanne going to waver. Half-heartedness was not an option.

Bible College

Not surprisingly Susanne's conversion was greeted with scepticism at home. 'Oh, you've got holy?' was her parents' only response.

Convinced she had joined a sect, they hoped this would just be a stage that would soon pass. Maybe this was simply a rebellious act of independence, they thought: she needed to get it out of her system before moving on with the rest of her life.

Her parents' attitude didn't upset Susanne though. In many ways she expected nothing less. They had never been interested in Christianity so why would they greet the news of their daughter's conversion with excitement?

Susanne was a bright girl, and yet as a new believer she knew little of God's Word or life under his rule. Some lifestyle changes were needed but as yet she was unaware that anything was wrong.

'I need to know my Bible better,' she decided. She was right of course, and although she was getting along to church regularly, she was hungry for more. 'I'll go to Bible college,' she thought. It seemed simple for this new Christian: the best place to learn more about God's word would be in a theological college. Anxious that this wasn't to be just another whimsical fantasy, Susanne spent months contemplating the move. The more she thought about it, the more sense it made to her.

There was a slight problem though. Susanne had become engaged to a man who was not a Christian. A crunch decision was needed: was she really prepared to give the Lord *everything* as she had previously promised? Would she forfeit her pending marriage for the sake of God and His call upon her life?

There were three of four portions of Scripture that were known to Susanne and special to her since her conversion a few months earlier. While on a youth weekend she turned to one of them.

> The word of the LORD came to me, saying,
> 'Before I formed you in the womb I knew you,
> before you were born I set you apart; I appointed you as a prophet to the nations.'
> 'Ah, Sovereign LORD,' I said, 'I do not know how to speak; I am only a child.'
> But the LORD said to me, 'Do not say, "I am only a child." You must go to everyone I send you to and say whatever I command you. Do not be afraid of them, for I am with you and will rescue you,' declares the LORD '. . . They will fight against you but will not overcome you, for I am with you and will rescue you,' declares the LORD (Jer. 1:4–8,19).

'I claimed these verses for myself. They felt so applicable, so real. My mother some years earlier had told me that if abortion had been as easy as it is today, then I would have been aborted at the first opportunity. But now I was reading how God Himself had brought me together, designed me and made me in my mum's body. I had a purpose and my life was not to be wasted. As I read and re-read those verses back to myself, I made a

conscious decision that I was not to marry my fiancé –
God had different plans for me – and I began my application to Bible college.'

Knowing very little about Bible colleges, Susanne
sought advice from Elisabeth. She had reservations
about some of the colleges, feeling they would not suit
Susanne's excitable personality. This could potentially
lead to problems. A giddy new Christian ready to push
boundaries, deliberately or otherwise, was not ideal.

'The first time I went to church following my conversion I wore my new tiny miniskirt. I really liked it. I was
so proud because I had made it myself. I found out later
that someone wanted to say something to me about how
inappropriate it was for church but my friend said, "No,
don't say anything to her yet." It was the best thing she
ever did because if someone had said something at that
stage, I would never have gone into a church again. It is
so important, if someone is a new believer, to just love
them and leave them (with regards to issues like dress).
They will find out on their own. And that is exactly what
I did – I found out on my own after a while, as it dawned
on me that perhaps it was best if my skirts got a bit
longer, and my T-shirts became not quite so revealing.'

While Susanne did not conform to the typical
Christian life expected of her, she was resolute as to
what she wanted to do. The Lord was number one in her
life and He was to come first, above all things. She was
not prepared to compromise; she would not waver. She
would have her own way of doing things, but before the
Lord she would not mess around.

Susanne's Journal

Father, I thank you for yesterday, for the confirmation that I received on Saturday evening and for the 'go' that I received. I take it as a confirmation for the Bible Foundation course . . .

. . . You, Lord, know all the answers to my questions. I look forward to this week of fasting and prayer and have great expectations. Lord, fill me with your Spirit, make my heart pure and free . . .

. . . Wait for the Spirit, be patient, believe in his capabilities and trust in him, that he will bring about God's will in his own way and time . . .

'Speak Lord, your servant is listening.'

Amen

'You must go to everyone I send you to and say whatever I command you. Do not be afraid of them, for I am with you' (Jer. 1:7,8)

'I knew my parents weren't going to be happy at my decision to go to Bible college and so I wasn't surprised by their reaction. They went crazy. They thought I had lost the plot and was throwing my life away to some fanatical, weird, money-grabbing sect. They said there and then that they wouldn't be giving me any support, financial or otherwise, for my studies, that I would be on my own and would have to fend for myself. A verse from Jeremiah 1 came into my mind . . . '

'They will fight against you but will not overcome you, for I am with you and will rescue you,' declares the LORD.

When her parents saw how strong her resolution was, their anger turned to fear. Who were this group that had control of their daughter so completely? What were they after, and what would they do to her?

Susanne, in her usual animated and fervent manner, phoned the college. One can only imagine the conversation she had, but from her end, she was in no doubt that she would be coming to the college as soon as was possible. The college tried to put the brakes on a little, suggesting that she completed and returned the application form before confidently announcing to them that she *would* be joining them.

Susanne didn't see the point of this formality. 'I don't need an application, the Lord told me I have to go, so I'm coming!' she repeated.

Still unconvinced, although impressed by her enthusiasm, the admissions secretary replied nervously, 'Yes, well, it's better that you come and talk to us beforehand.'

Susanne laughed and replied 'OK, so what do you want to know?'

They would get used to this style of conversation with Susanne, but they would also grow to love her.

Following her pastor's eventual approval of her application (he was sceptical that after being a Christian for such a short period she would want to attend Bible college), Susanne arrived at the New Life Bible School in Walzenhausen, Switzerland, for her three-month course.

As an intelligent and sharp-minded girl, she was like a sponge soaking up all she was taught. The end of her course came quickly (though just at the right time, before her money dried up completely).

It was then that the school advisors sat down with her over coffee and pleaded with her to stay on for their three-year course. Susanne had been an excellent student. She had not lost her blunt nature and frequently mischievous personality, but they liked her. They saw potential in this young Christian; they believed she could be of great use to the Lord.

Although she was interested, there were some major doubts for Susanne to overcome first. It was the same old problem: finances. No money was available from home, so if she was going to stay on a miracle was needed.

'Don't worry, the Lord will look after it,' the college leaders told her. She thought they were crazy. Although previously confident that this was the place she should be, difficulties with money were making her anxious. She couldn't even imagine how it could work. She had been brought up in a family where money mattered, and just going ahead and trusting it would come seemed foolhardy and reckless.

The college was not about to let Susanne go due to a lack of trust in God on her part, though. They read to her Matthew 6:33

> But seek first his kingdom and his righteousness, and all these things will be given to you as well.

One of the leaders said 'If you believe in this, trust the Lord, He will provide.'

She looked at him. 'It's easy for me to trust the Lord, but if you don't get the money . . .' She thought a little about what she had just said and the contradiction between the words 'trust' and 'but'. It was crazy but she decided she would stay for three years and, if the money came, it would confirm she was doing the right thing.

'Lord,' she prayed, 'if You have an idea how this can work, I will stay three years.'

There were no dramatic miracles: no winning lottery ticket slipped under her door; no huge gift that would sort her out for the remainder of the course. Instead, at just the right moment, every time, a small but precise gift for the required amount made its way to Susanne's pocket one way or another. Susanne was thrilled. The Lord was further confirming she was in His place, at His time.

Class Elections

Susanne's friend had suggested that the New Life Bible School would suit her better than other, more conservative colleges. They may have been more relaxed with regards to legalistic rules and regulations, but this was certainly no holiday camp. College life consisted of two main teaching areas. First, unsurprisingly, the students were taught the Bible in the usual classroom format. However, they were also required to take lifestyle modules that addressed the way of life for Christian disciples, something Susanne *really* loved.

'Our day started at 5.30 a.m. and usually didn't finish until after 10 p.m. We certainly got a lot done. When I first saw the timetable, I was pleased, as I like to keep busy.'

It was certainly great training for future years on a busy mission field. Long days would become part and parcel of everyday life for Susanne. The curriculum only allowed for two weekends off a year, and contained an eight-month placement in addition to a nine-week mission trip to Zaire. It didn't allow much time for students to go home, not that this concerned Susanne in the slightest. Her parents had made their views clear.

While in Zaire with a major missions organization, Susanne saw many special places. 'I had read numerous books that had been written about the rainforests where we were staying. I was now experiencing these places first hand. I re-read many of the books when I returned home: being able to picture the places easily helped me to fully appreciate the missionaries' stories.'

Once the trip came to an end, they returned to their base in Switzerland. There something special happened to Susanne.

The college, as so many do, was holding class elections for its student representative. There were two candidates standing, Susanne and another girl. Both were excellent choices and it was too close to call who would win the final vote of confidence from their class peers. It was so close, in fact, that they just couldn't decide whom to elect. As would seem appropriate for a Bible college election, the nominees were asked to return to their rooms and prayerfully consider if the position was for them. The two of them did so, going their separate ways to their individual bedrooms.

Being a relatively new Christian of just over a year, Susanne wasn't too sure what to do.

She did the only sensible thing: she got on her knees and began to talk with the Lord.

'Dear heavenly Father . . .' She paused when she realized she didn't know what to say. What is one meant to pray in a situation such as this?

Susanne turned to her Bible and allowed it to fall open randomly. Isaiah 60 was in front of her. As she began to read, she realized that she didn't mind whether she was to be the leader or not.

> Arise, shine, for your light has come,
> and the glory of the LORD rises upon you.
> See, darkness covers the earth
> and thick darkness is over the peoples,

but the LORD rises upon you
and his glory appears over you.
Nations will come to your light,
and kings to the brightness of your dawn.
Lift up your eyes and look about you:
All assemble and come to you;
your sons will come from afar,
and your daughters are carried on the arm.

'At this time I didn't know what that would mean to me; I couldn't understand and I didn't know that it was actually for Zion – as a naïve, new believer, I just took it for me personally. I thought "OK, this is too much for me; it's too big." I couldn't understand what the Lord was telling me. I knew at that point that I shouldn't be the leader of the class. I just knew the Lord had something else for me. I let the others know and the other girl became class representative.'

Without Susanne's knowledge, a girl had begun to pray for her daily a few weeks before. She was at Bible college with Susanne and the Lord had laid a burning desire upon her heart to pray for her friend. Her specific prayer was that God would, in His time, lead her to work in a Muslim country. Which one didn't matter, she just longed that Susanne would go one day. She told Susanne, who found the idea of someone specifically praying for her a little strange.

She found it even more strange when the school announced it was having a week of prayer and fasting. 'Crazy,' she thought, 'they are all crazy!' She was prepared to go along with it though and gladly joined in with this 'crazy' bunch she had grown to love so much.

'My praying friend gave me a book at the end of the week and asked me to read it. It was called *Too Hard for God*, written by Charles Marsh. The people whose lives were described in it were remarkably so protected by God that even poisonous food did not kill them. For someone like me, who considered the concept of talking with God strange, it was incredible for Him to answer the requests of His children in such a way. I was like a giddy child, eating sweets or ice cream for the very first time. I wanted to know more. I wanted more. I wanted answers, miraculous answers, to prayer like that, in my life.'

Over the following weeks of that month in 1988, the need for Christian believers to be reaching out to Muslims continued to come up time and time again. Susanne was beginning to sense a love and a longing for these people. It wasn't for another two months, though, when the college was holding another week of prayer and fasting, that Susanne's desires were confirmed. Following her baptism later on that week, she felt convicted that in time she was indeed to go and reach this lost group. Her enthusiasm and desire to work with Muslims in the east was sealed. It was the beginning of a new era.

A New Era

Although desperately aware of her call from God, there was much Susanne needed to do first. She had next to no money, absolutely no support from home, and for a single woman to work in a Muslim country would be difficult. If she were going to work abroad, in whatever country, she would need more preparation, prayer and resources.

'My next steps were really up to me. I had a big blank map of Germany in front of me. I was prepared to go anywhere. There was no country I was particularly attached to. The more I looked in Germany though, the more frustrated I became, as I couldn't find anything suitable. I began to look at opportunities outside of Germany. There was a friend of mine whom I got on really well with – the pastor in Rorschach, where I did my internship previously. I phoned him and asked for some help. Immediately he suggested a church. He said, 'You should go to Lindau. There is a church that the college has set up – they need somebody like you.'

Susanne wasn't sure she should ask what he meant as she might not have liked the answer. But her intrigue got the better of her and she asked for an explanation of what he meant by 'somebody like you'. He wasn't prepared to give an answer. Instead he challenged her to go out there and find out for herself.

'I had always seen the lights of this little island across Lake Constance from my bedroom at college. I would look out at it at night with curiosity, wondering who lived there and what went on upon that little island. Now I was going to find out! Over the years I had collected many, many belongings and so I began the long job of packing. With my bags in hand I headed off to the church in Lindau on the far side of the lake. This was to be my new home. I had a tiny sink, a toilet, and a Sunday school room (during the week). That was it.'

Due to the goodness of God, this was no real problem for Susanne. While she took care of herself, luxurious accommodation was not required to keep her happy. At times she wished for a larger place, a place of her own, to spread her things about in. However, she was content and got on with the job in hand.

After a struggle to get any employment from the job centre (they viewed her as homeless) Susanne was given work. It was a simple picking, packing and delivering job for a wholesaler but she enjoyed it. Her little rusty bike, with its squeaky brakes, carried her to and from work each day. There were no career prospects and she knew this wasn't a long-term commitment, but rather a stopgap for things to come. Things were about to start, although she was unaware of them . . .

Meeting Tilmann

New Life was an independent church of around fifty people. The Bible college had planted it some months before Susanne's arrival. As she camped down in the building and became acquainted with her surroundings, she was still none the wiser as to why she would be 'good for the church'. Trying to find out, she offered her assistance to the two part-time pastors. She was just out of Bible college and keen to get stuck into the day-to-day work of a Christian servant. Susanne was left somewhat surprised as they rebuffed her offer, telling her just to 'sit tight' for a while and see what happened.

'I was a little put out. It seemed a funny thing to say. Here I was offering to help out, in whatever way they wanted, and they were telling me to just relax a little bit and see what was going on. Normally churches are desperate for help and will welcome with open arms anyone offering.'

Some weeks later, although they felt like months to Susanne, she returned to the pastors and asked if she could start a bookstall in the church. She'd noticed that they currently didn't have anything like this and she thought they should. This was the reason she was needed here. This was what the Bible college teacher meant when he said 'They could use someone like you.' Susanne was a servant, who would go under the direction of the leadership but would not drift along. Her innovative and creative character wouldn't allow it.

The bookstall was a success and the congregation found the books helpful to their faith. Susanne wasn't finished, though. In the locality there were many locals whom she was desperate to reach – her heart burned for them. She joined a German guy from a church in nearby Austria, beginning a club for the children of refugees each week. All age groups from toddlers to teenagers came along. You can imagine the noise that a group of this age would make and the community weren't that happy at first. Susanne got a small communal room, with bright green walls, in the basement of an apartment block. Tables and chairs were all they had, but it was enough to get by. The caretaker of the property was sceptical that the club would ever take off and allowed the usage of the room to humour them. With a term or so under their belt, the group became more and more popular. Seeing the growing popularity of the club, the caretaker was only too glad to allow them to use the room – and the community were pleased.

Susanne's Journal

*'Ask of me [says the Lord],
and I will make the nations your inheritance, the ends of the earth your possession'
(Ps. 2:8).*

. . . Lord I ask you for the nations!

Is anything impossible for God? No! I thank you Lord that with you all is possible. Am I afraid of death, of dying for Christ? Lord thank you for the confidence that your child need not be afraid of death and that with this knowledge in my head and my heart, I may go your way.

Susanne's work didn't go unnoticed. The pastors were glad of her help and she was beginning to have an impact upon the church and the surrounding area. One of them was especially thankful for her arrival. His name was Tilmann Geske. Part-time pastor, part-time fork-lift driver in a warehouse, Tilmann began to fall in love with Susanne.

'This guy is embarrassing,' she wrote in her journal shortly after meeting him for the first time. 'He just mumbles all the time. I can't understand what he is saying. And his haircut is awful. It looks like someone has put a bowl on his head and just cut around it – plus it's so thick.'

Susanne can remember like yesterday the first time she laid eyes on the quirky-looking Tilmann. He was tall, with a moustache and chunky glasses. He was playing the guitar at the front of church, dressed in clothes only a hippy would wear.

'What kind of guy would be like this? This is awful and so embarrassing!' Susanne recalls. 'I really didn't like him. From the first moment we met, I thought he was unbelievable. I went along to the prayer meetings so I would see him quite a lot. I couldn't understand his prayers though as he would just mumble on. All of a sudden the room would fall silent and it was only then that we knew, OK, Tilmann has finished! I hated it.'

By coincidence, the two of them were placed in the same home group. Susanne wasn't going to escape that easily. As she says, she had to 'survive this guy' a little longer.

It got worse; the two of them were helping to rearrange a room in church – it was Susanne's worst nightmare. 'I couldn't even bear be in the same room as this guy. He really freaked me out! I did my best to avoid him but it just didn't happen. I had no clue that he might like me at this stage, but to be honest I didn't care. I liked a guy from another town in Switzerland, so Tilmann didn't even enter into my head romantically. That is, until the other pastor started teasing me about him. "Oh he's a lovely guy . . ." he would say. My usual response was "Yes, but not for me . . ." He didn't listen to my brushing off though, and carried on regardless.'

Susanne's Journal

Lord, I thank you for all that I was able to experience today, of how you guided.

Lord, teach me to be quiet before you and to wait for you.

Lord, you see the thoughts and feelings that keep me awake, which I don't know how to handle. What shall I do about Tilmann? At the moment I feel completely confused.

Lord, I don't know what I expect from him. On the one hand I am scared that he will fall in love with me, on the other hand I like being near him. Totally mad?!

Lord, your thoughts are higher than my thoughts and your ways are different to my ways. I thank you that you are my shelter: that you take all my worries, fears and problems from me and help me to solve them.

I love you Lord.

Amen

'I have got something to ask you . . .'

Tilmann Geske was shy. He kept himself to himself. Diligent and hardworking, he was a dab hand at all things practical. When it came to romantic matters he certainly wasn't very forthcoming. However, he knew he had fallen for this blue-eyed girl. After several weeks of convincing himself it was a sensible thing to do, he wrote Susanne a letter expressing his feelings for her. She was away on a camp a few hundred miles away, so he reasoned that it was the safest place for her to receive the card – hundreds of miles from where he was.

On her return, when Susanne failed to even mention the card, Tilmann plucked up the courage to ask her about it. Unfortunately for him, the card never arrived.

'Looking back at the situation,' Susanne recalls now, 'it was good it didn't get to me. Had I received and read the card at that time, I would have freaked out. It wouldn't have gone down well at all. The Lord definitely was in that sequence of events.'

Despite the instinctive repulsion she felt at Tilmann's advances, a change was beginning to happen in her attitude towards him.

She was beginning to get fed up with the living conditions in the church so she decided to move. She found a tiny room in a house with an elderly lady. It wasn't ideal. There was no heating system and she had to share the bathroom with the landlady. Before long, Susanne was back at the church, staying the occasional night.

'When winter came, it was freezing cold in my little room. So I started to sleep back in the church because it was warmer. I would think to myself "What is the point in cycling up to church in the morning for morning prayer; I might as well just stay up there."'

Tilmann would be out driving the fork-lift in the afternoon, so he got down to church early in the morning to start his church work. With Susanne down there too, the two of them would often eat breakfast together. For a shy man, Tilmann did very well.

'He would always ask me personal and therefore quite odd questions. He would quiz me about my future, my desires and plans. And then he would go on about what he hoped to do, how he wanted to learn the piano and things. He didn't realize that I wasn't interested but I hadn't understood he was asking me and talking to me in this way because he was in love with me.'

Susanne and Tilmann were spending more and more time together. She would often ask to borrow his car to travel to her new job at the pottery; he was only too pleased to help.

In November, Tilmann and Susanne found themselves together again, this time on a weekend church retreat in a town a couple of hours away. There were two cars from New Life travelling to the event. For the first time Susanne realized she might be falling for this mumbling pastor, whom she had dismissed for so long. She was extremely disappointed she couldn't travel in his car to the weekend resort. It wasn't a long journey but she was learning the hard lesson that she wanted to spend more and more time with Tilmann.

'It suddenly dawned on me that I might actually really like this guy. I stopped what I was doing and began to pray: "Please Lord, please. Not Tilmann, please don't let me fall in love with him. What are you doing here God?"'

Perhaps not the most theologically intellectual prayer she had ever prayed but she was desperate; desperate not to fall in love with someone so funny! Desperate or not, the Lord was dealing with her feelings, and He was going to have His way, however long it took.

Susanne was joining friends at the Bible college for another week of prayer and fasting, after the church retreat ended. It dawned on her that she would need to borrow Tilmann's spare car again. As he dropped her off, she turned to him and said, nervous due to the frequency of her asking, 'I have something to ask you.'

To her surprise he replied, 'Me too!'

Unsure of what he was going to say, she volunteered to go first. 'Please can I borrow your car again?' Tilmann agreed immediately. Right now she could have asked for anything and he would have agreed.

'OK, so what about your question?' Susanne replied quickly, almost forgetting to thank him for his generous loan.

'He ummed and erred for a while' Susanne recalls 'and I was getting impatient. He clearly didn't realise I had things to get on and do and I was watching the clock.'

'Tilmann, I need to get on and pack before I go away . . .'

He cut to the chase: 'Do you want to marry me?' he blurted out, looking directly into her eyes.

Taken aback, Susanne replied in the only way she knew how. 'OK, I have three clauses that any potential husband needs to fulfil. One, you have to be a believer; two, you have to have been a believer longer than me; and three, I want to live in a Muslim country.'

She felt certain the final point would prove a stumbling block; too much even for a man in love. She waited for his reply.

'Oh, this is fine with me!' he replied with no hesitation. Susanne was shell-shocked.

Suddenly the rush to get home wasn't so pressing. Tilmann shared with Susanne how he'd been in Indonesia and had always wanted to go to a Muslim country, but first he wanted to spend time working in a church. She conceded he wasn't just pulling her leg; he *actually* did want to go and reach Muslims in their own land.

They went their separate ways, without so much as a hug, but instead Susanne committed herself to praying the offer over in the coming week of prayer and fasting. She would return to him in seven days with her answer.

'I found out some time later that Tilmann had been trying to ask me this crucial question for the last four weeks but the appropriate time never arose. Looking back on it, I was glad he couldn't, because I would have rejected him there and then. I wasn't ready to hear his question until the actual moment he asked. As I promised, I went away and prayed about it, but after just one day I realized that this was really from the Lord. It was so clear; it wasn't really my decision because if it was, I would have never decided to marry Tilmann. But God brought the pieces together and I wanted to do His will. I had always, of course, prayed for the right man to pop up but always believed that there was no one, truly no one, for me. I had nothing to say against Tilmann's proposal, there was no reason to reject him and I felt God leading me to him.'

Susanne and Tilmann didn't speak for another week, although her decision was already made. She held to her commitment and kept praying for a clear leading from God. She experienced a complete peace about the whole situation which she knew could only come from God – and this led her to believe she was ready to accept the proposal.

Susanne's Journal

Thank you Lord for giving me ever more certainty that Tilmann is the man for me . . .

Thank you that I can see the inner beauty of Tilmann and that I feel drawn to him. It is your biggest gift to me: that you have given me someone by my side who is interested in me, in the person I keep partly (or rather, almost always) hidden behind a thick wall. Thank you that this wall has now got a big crack in it.

You know my fears about a real, deep relationship. Help me to be honest and to trust you. Help me to open up and to have no fear of being honest and open about feelings. I am scared of being hurt again. I wish for a marriage as you intended marriage to be, and I would like to be a wife of your heart . . .

Lord, I thank you for the unending joy you give me. It is wonderful to be in love. Thank you that Tilmann is not as passionate and daring as I. He is my brake and it is good that way.

Thank you for your daily help.

Amen

A month later, on Boxing Day 1991, the two of them were engaged. They didn't date like an American or English couple would, but rather they saw each other at church and spoke there when they could.

But what about his awful hair and clothes? Did Susanne step in and sort him out?

'Actually I didn't say anything about his hair. He had a haircut before we married, so maybe his friend and co-pastor Tomas told him to sort himself out!'

Susanne wasn't going to be so subtle about his dress sense though. 'The only thing I really remember is that after we were married I talked to him about his dreadful clothes. He would always wear brown jumpers or shirts. I hate brown. In fact it shouldn't even be called a colour; you wear black, white and then all the other colours but not brown! Then I started to see what stuff he wore and I would look to see if he had worn it over the past year. If he hadn't I would give it away or throw it out. It just filled up space. So slowly but surely all the brown stuff went out.'

'He hated to buy things for himself. If he went shopping for clothes, someone would have to go with him. When we found a suitable jumper or shirt or something, we would then have to force him to actually buy it.'

'He was quite prudent with money, not wanting to waste any on belongings he didn't feel he needed. Even when he did need new things, Tilmann always saw others with greater need as his priority.'

❀　　❀　　❀　　❀

Susanne's parents were still unsupportive of her life – and particularly her faith. The day after Susanne and Tilmann's official engagement they drove to her parents; Susanne called her father and warned him that she was bringing a 'friend' with her to 'show' them. Partial to a drink, her father was quite drunk when they arrived. He uttered the worst possible things a man could possibly say to another human being and of course Susanne was hurt. However, she was determined to be resolute and strong. She replied, 'Actually, you can't say anything against us because we're engaged. So forget about it!' Her dad retaliated with even more verbal abuse – but she had said what she thought.

They stayed just one night before 'escaping'.

Susanne's Journal

'The Lord knows those who are his,'
  2 Timothy 2:19

God knows me through and through. He knows everything that I need; better than I know myself. Thank you, Lord, for giving me Tilmann. I consider him as coming directly from you. I would like to place this relationship under your protection and ask what you would like, even in this area . . .

Thank you, Lord, for Tilmann. He is a great comfort. Thank you that you have given me a view of what is to come, for that was just the beginning. It will be a steep and bumpy road, but with a clear goal before our eyes.

Lord, I thank you for Tilmann. I am so pleased that you granted him his wish for a wife. We are getting to know each other bit by bit and are discovering how to work together. It is clear that we are very different but it is fascinating how much we have in common.

Lord, I see your work and guidance. Thank you that Tilmann wants to marry me. I can barely imagine what it will be like but I am so happy. I have a real deep peace about it. Yesterday he told his mother and I told my mother about it. Oh Lord, I am so happy!

I love you Lord.

                                        Amen

Turkey Calling

Tilmann Geske and Susanne Beuter became Mr and Mrs Tilmann Geske on 20 June 1992, still without the support of Susanne's family (though they did attend the wedding). Tilmann's family weren't all believers but they were at least supportive of the marriage.

Tilmann was contracted to complete five years of pastoral work at New Life (which became an FEG church during that time[1]) before they could move to their dream destination – an Islamic nation. So in the three years that remained, the two prayerfully considered where God was leading them. They asked the Lord as the Bible commands, seeking His direction.

Each morning of their married lives, before either of them left for work or began their duties of the day, they would pray together. They would talk through the issues facing them in the coming hours and the contacts that they would sharing with, before bowing their heads to talk with God. These times together before the Lord were precious.

They were not entirely in agreement though. Tilmann was keen to return to Indonesia while Susanne had her heart set on Turkey. Because of their indecision and lack of common confidence with regards to their future, they decided to leave it a little longer before making plans.

They hoped that somehow they would both find some common ground, somewhere that they could both settle upon.

Two significant events then took place that were going to be instrumental in their future. The first led to the second. The two of them began praying for what seemed a logical location, Iran. It was situated somewhat between the two countries but appeared to be the answer to their desire to work with Muslims. After several weeks of prayer, they heard about a friend of theirs from Bible college who was organizing a trip to Iran. They expressed an interest in joining him and before long they were invited along.

Running parallel to these events was God's larger plan. For several months they had been receiving the newsletter of a Swiss friend who also had similar passions to them. Both Tilmann and Susanne would, independently, spend time reading and praying through their brother's news and concerns.

'We were praying very much for the impending exploration to Iran. Neither of us wanted to do something that was not God's will, so we continued to seek His mind about it. And He was beginning to warn us that this might not be the right thing. We were four people short for the trip and we wouldn't be going if the right people weren't found to come with us. We did all we could and trusted the Lord that His will would be done, as it says in Matthew 6. It was about this time that we got the latest prayer news from our Swiss friend. Enclosed with the letter was a flyer advertising a prayer journey through eastern Turkey later that year. This obviously caught my eye and really interested me but I didn't mention anything to Tilmann, as I didn't want him to feel under any pressure. Then, out of the blue, one Saturday morning Tilmann asked me, "Have you read this prayer letter?" as he handed it to me. I told him I had.'

"There was something interesting in there," he said.

I acted surprised and replied, "Oh, what was it?"

"Yes, they have a prayer journey in east Turkey . . ."

As we talked about it, it became clear that he had the same idea as I had, that we were keener to do this trip than go to Iran. Although we had prayed about it I was still amazed because this was what I wanted to do and Tilmann thought the same for himself.'

The very next day the Iranian trip leader phoned. They were anxious about how he would take their news that they were going to drop out. They didn't need to worry though: he was calling to say that the journey had been cancelled as not enough people had been recruited.

The call confirmed that the trip to Turkey was what the Lord really wanted. Pleased that they had trusted God and not their own plans, they prepared to leave for their adventure.

First Thoughts

'When we went on our honeymoon we took a car through the Greek islands and ended up in Istanbul. We spent at least a week there, walking and taking in the culture. We experienced many deep emotions, all brought on by the sights, sounds, food and atmosphere.'

'We took a boat trip where onboard there was a totally lovely family. The mother was dressed in a chador[2] – but the way she treated their kids and they spoke to one another as a family was really lovely. Tilmann turned to me and said, "You know, I think I could work among these people!" That was the first real step in the direction of possible going to Turkey.'

'Our prayer-journey trip was a bit of a disaster. We both got quite ill and that naturally put a dampener on the whole experience – having said that I loved the country right away. Our time there was a real spiritual battle, which was good preparation for the future. I was pregnant, in my second or third month, and had been sick practically since conception. One day I would be better, the next day worse, and Tilmann also had a bug. We were really ill, lying in bed, not moving anywhere. We travelled through some of the major cities like Istanbul, Mersin and Urfa. Others, like Bitilis, we had to avoid due to the dangers to our safety. We moved toward the border with Iran and then back to Istanbul. During the whole trip either Tilmann or I were ill. The company who took us thought we would never come back to Turkey again because our experience was so horrific. My condition was so bad that the only thing I could eat was baby food – which we discovered my body could handle. It was my last and only option – if I hadn't eaten anything I would have needed hospital treatment. Tilmann always had to carry me as I was too weak to walk. Having said all of this, I wasn't scared at all, even when we couldn't go to places for security reasons. I was just aware that it was the evil one trying to make us really mad; he was trying to make sure we wouldn't come back. It just made me more resolute though. I thought to myself, "OK, you can take whatever you want from us but we're going to come back." I was like a stubborn child.'

'At that time we were arranging to make contact with Hans [not his real name], the man from the prayer letter. He was from an organization that we would later work with, although we didn't know that at that time. It was late autumn and Michal, our eldest, wasn't born yet. Once again, we felt like the evil one was doing his best to stop us going anywhere. Trying to stop us exploring the Lord's will. We had bought a second-hand car. It wasn't the best car you'll ever see but it was sturdy and reliable, which is what we needed. We drove to Lake Constance to meet Hans but stopped off for a bite to eat before we arrived. All of sudden nothing in the car would work. It wouldn't go backwards or forwards and neither would the gears work. It was completely done for. So with me being heavily pregnant, and Tilmann tired from driving, we had to push the car into a safe place where we could stop.

'We were so keen to get to our 4 p.m. appointment that we decided to catch the train. The trains in Switzerland are not the most direct, so we were going to be a bit late, but we thought we should try to make it. We gave Hans a call and he kindly made all the arrangements at his end to come and get us from the station. I was so glad we made the effort to get there. We had a good talk and our partnership in the work became clearer the more we talked. He advised us that we should start going to the organization's training base in Germany and begin our preparation for arriving on the field. We were grateful for the helpful suggestion.

'As we made our way back to Germany after our train ride, we prayed regarding the situation with the car, not knowing what we'd do if it still didn't work. Our powerful God did wonderful things: we got into the car and it worked perfectly first time! It was like the scene in Frank Peretti's book, *Present Darkness*. There is one point in the story where the angel of the Lord puts a sword in the car so that it doesn't work and then he pulls it out again. We felt just the same.'

Training Starts

Keen to get started, Tilmann and Susanne began the thorough process of application for the field. While that did not take much time, the months of training that followed seemed to drag.

They went to study in Bournemouth (on the south coast of England), taking their place at the Christian English Language Centre. Susanne was pregnant once again, with their second child, Lukas. Unfortunately, they were going to have to spend some time apart as Tilmann needed to complete his Teaching English as a Foreign Language course. So, after watching Germany beat England in the Euro '96 finals together, they said goodbye to each other for twelve weeks. Susanne headed home in the car with Michal, their first-born.

Once home, Susanne began the long process of packing up their belongings. They needed time to get ready. Then Tilmann returned from England so the two of them could take part in the final candidates' course, which in Germany lasts six months.

In many ways it seemed a long time. Another six months of study; another six months before they could get on with the job. However, in the end it went fairly quickly. There was much to cram into a short space of time. They were taught many life skills that they would need in the field. Susanne and Tilmann took all their classes together, which provided much fuel for conversation.

They attended all sorts of interesting meetings, ranging from anything such as looking after children in the field to cross-cultural ministry. The organization wanted its employees as ready as they could be for what they were about to experience.

'We had to read a bunch of books before we could progress with our work. Naturally we needed to know the history of our organization, its work and its mission. We were told we had to read books on church planting in preparation for our ministry in Turkey but I really didn't enjoy it. It was hard work. I would try and do two things at once to make it more bearable – usually while feeding Lukas.'

Towards the end of this period, the couple needed to tell Susanne's family of their plans.

Susanne recalls, 'To be honest, I didn't really mind what they thought. I just told them, we're going to Turkey and that was it. We left it very low-key. I didn't go into any detail about which organization we were going with – there was no point. We just explained that we wanted to live in another country and that Tilmann wanted to open up a business as an English teacher. We were scared that if we told them more they would mix up things. We were going to be part of an organization, in Turkey, that was part of another very sensitive organization, so we had to be careful. I didn't have a good relationship with them, so it wasn't difficult not to talk to them about these things.'

One final requirement was needed before they were confirmed to go – to pass the organization's interview. The two of them were interviewed together as a couple and their situation discussed.

'To our delight we were accepted as workers and on 25 January 1997, Tilmann, I and the children were commissioned to leave for the Turkish mission field. At the service they gave me a verse that I remember to this day. It was John 15:16. "You did not choose me but I chose you and appointed you to go and bear fruit – fruit that will last." Michal and Lukas were given a verse from Proverbs 14 – a verse that has become really special to us in recent months.'

> He who fears the LORD has a secure fortress,
> and for his children it will be a refuge.

In Transit

It was a warm Saturday morning in September. Tilmann, Susanne, Michal and eleven-month-old Lukas were getting ready to leave Germany for their new home in central Turkey. They were keen to settle as far east as they could, as there were few Christians there. Adana was the furthest their organization would let them go for their initial time as workers in their new homeland.

Tilmann had done some scouting around for a suitable vehicle to transport them across Europe to Turkey. After some looking and even more negotiation, he managed to find a Turkish van. (During a labour shortage in the fifties and sixties, the German government signed recruitment agreements with several states including Turkey: this led to many Turkish workers living in Germany.) It was perfect for what they needed – big enough to carry all their belongings, with previous Turkish owners as a bonus. Tilmann came out of his shy, retiring shell for a moment, managing to negotiate a price of 1000 German marks (about £300). It was just about roadworthy for the journey and they were thrilled.

And so the loading began. Bags of all shapes and sizes, colours and descriptions were packed systematically into the van. Sewing machines, a computer,

Tilmann's DIY kit – all added to the number of things being bundled into the van. The little furniture they owned was loaded in too and, before long, the doors were slammed shut: absolutely nothing more could fit in. Tilmann and Michal would go by road, while Susanne and the baby would follow by plane.

The journey was going to be tiring and demanding for all of them. The van went by boat to Antalya in southwest Turkey and then they drove across to their destination, Adana. The long and bumpy journey proved to be one of the beautiful times in Michal's life that she spent with her father: something that will never leave her. They laughed and joked as they always did, Michal proving a good companion for Tilmann on what would have otherwise been a lonely four-day journey.

Meanwhile, poor Susanne was pushing a trolley through the airport with any number of extra bags that she either couldn't do without, or just wouldn't fit in the van, while also carrying Lukas on her hip. He was not a happy baby. Airports aren't ideal places for young children; not least, when you have just left home and Dad and sister are nowhere to be seen. The poor chap didn't understand what was happening.

His tears and screams just made life that little bit harder for Susanne, who was already beginning to fear the excess baggage charge that would be coming her way any minute.

'I prayed many quick and quiet prayers that day. I had no money, cash or otherwise – just my ticket. My bags were in excess of the 30-kilo weight limit by over double. There was no way I was going to be let off this amount of luggage and I was worried as to what I would do.'

Susanne's flight was called forward for checking in. She made her way into the queue, with Lukas still clinging to her.

She was about halfway down the line, when a plane attendant approached her.

'Is this all your luggage?' he asked.

Fearful of the impending doom her answer would bring, Susanne agreed with some trepidation.

Seeing the surprised look on the attendant's face, she explained that she and her family were moving to Turkey.

'OK, come with me,' the gentleman responded in a surprisingly calm manner.

'I don't know how many bags or kilos went through with me that day, but I know for sure that I was way over the allowed limit. The bags kept coming and were processed through the system. When they had all gone through, I asked the attendant how much that would cost me, knowing full well I had nothing to pay him with. He replied "Nothing." I couldn't believe it. I was so far over the limit it was unreal, but the Lord had heard my cry. He ushered us through, and Lukas and I boarded the plane. Praise the Lord!'

Adana – in Black and White

Life in Adana was very different to what they were used to but Susanne and Tilmann settled in quickly. With their hearts so fixed on reaching the Turks they were determined that the struggles of language and culture, which would inevitably come their way, would not deter them from their calling.

This was easier for Susanne than Tilmann. For the first time in his life, his home was his office. This took some adjustment but he wasn't keen. As soon as another venue became available, he signed the appropriate papers so that he could move out and have his own working space away from the noisy house. He was then able to enjoy arriving home and to relax, without feeling the compelling call from his desk in the corner.

With some books in the old Ottoman Turkish language, Tilmann and Susanne set about mastering Turkish. Tilmann came from a family of linguists – his mother taught the children various languages well into her eighties – and so he quickly began to grasp the basics. (Tilmann's ability with languages was so good that he studied Greek and Hebrew at college. From then on he read his daily devotions from the original Greek.) For Susanne, it took a little longer, not least because during her second year of study, she became pregnant for the third time, with Miriam.

A small Turkish house church had been established a while before the Geskes' arrival. However, being 'foreigners' they couldn't join in right away. Instead they met with the small team of other workers in the area and ran a parallel church, rotating around each other's homes. It can be a lonely time, being far from home, working in another country, so Tilmann and Susanne found it a great blessing and help to have 'colleagues' in the local vicinity. These precious times spent together were happy – a real encouragement.

Susanne remembers the laboursome task of those first two years. 'We had no choice but to spend time learning the language and getting accustomed to Turkish culture. It was hard, and at times it got so frustrating. When you aren't picking up the language as quickly as you would like or you have to learn about the technical structure of the vocabulary, it can be easy to give up. At times like this, you have to remind yourself why you are doing it; you have to remind yourself it is worth it.'

Until they had adapted to the culture and had a firm grasp of the language they would remain total outsiders, unable to connect with the Turkish church. This was the perfect stimulus for them.

'I never really experienced any culture shock,' Susanne remembers cheerfully, before pausing. As she looks back, she does recall some things that took a bit of adapting to: 'Sometimes you sense that things are not as nice. For example, when you realize someone has lied to you, or they have exploited you because you are foreign. This can take some getting used to.'

On further reflection, Susanne doubts that deep down you ever get used to it: the unrelenting stares, honking of car horns 24/7, the call to prayer blaring out five times daily from the local mosque. Even the simplest tasks like buying food or preparing a meal seemed to take twice as long. Some women were veiled from head to toe, in contrast to others who enjoyed dressing like their Western role models on MTV. Many of the women Susanne met in the streets must have found it hard to comprehend the freedoms she enjoyed: a passport that could take her anywhere in the world she wanted and a supportive husband who trusted her and encouraged her to live life to the full. Injustice always irritates, especially when it is a regular occurrence.

Although reasonably settled, Tilmann found his new life in Turkey arduous. He was a quiet man who liked to get his head down and do the job, and do it well. He was extremely thorough and gave 100 per cent in everything he did.

Susanne remembers one time when Tilmann got especially irate.

'Usually Tilmann wouldn't talk too much, but one day he arrived home from work and immediately began talking – almost shouting. Because he was very much a perfectionist, when others produced sloppy work it would vex him terribly. On this particular day he arrived home totally disheartened. "These kids don't want to learn," he started, "and it's so frustrating . . . They know nothing after having so many years of English in class. What do I tell the parents? Your child knows nothing! They won't stand for that. My boss wants me to just say they are great so they will stay at the school, but I won't do that." My husband might have been quiet, but he did not lack passion for doing things correctly.'

❀   ❀   ❀   ❀

After spending two years in the 'foreign' church, suddenly, almost out of nowhere, it seemed that God wanted things to change. The two team leaders of the church left in the summer, returning to their home country, Canada. Their departure left Tilmann and Susanne in charge of the small group, though they didn't accept sole responsibility – they preferred to work with their colleagues than charge ahead alone.

It wasn't too long before a family joined them from Germany, and they formed what seemed like, in Susanne's words, 'a little German workers club'. From there other foreigners joined them which broke up the party, but it provided the opportunity to hold an 'International Sunday' in their house. At this stage there were still Turks coming along each week.

'Praise the Lord though, our house became too small for this and we needed to move it to our friend's home as they had more room. There would usually be around twenty people. We could sometimes have even more though, perhaps when groups visited on mission trips, particularly from America. We weren't too keen on having more foreigners come to our services as it doesn't always help, but it happened and we got on with it.'

The workers weren't completely cut off from their Turkish brothers and sisters though. Each month, on a Friday, they would share a special time of prayer together. It was time for spurring one another on as each one had the opportunity to share what they had been able to do during the last few weeks. One particular month, the Turkish church shared about their need for a bigger building to meet in, unaware that the 'foreign' church had the same dilemma. Their current facilities were no longer sufficient.

'They asked us if we would like to share a building with them. It was excellent. One of us would have our service in the morning and the other in the afternoon. Perfect. We agreed, and got on to it right away. We found a nice building that we could rent and, with a bit of work on it, we made it really nice. Tilmann, who was quite competent at DIY, did a super job with it. He was always good at drawing things and measuring, thinking through ideas. And so, by January 2000, it had developed into a fully established church. The landlord knew it was going to be used for a church, but didn't ask too many other questions about it, and he was fine. What is more, we had the added bonus of it being detached from any other houses, so we didn't have to ask permission from the neighbours. It was a perfect provision from the Lord for both congregations.'

Susanne was a hard worker, enhanced by her partner-ship with her talented husband. She worked hard at building relationships with her neighbours. So often, their contact revolved around the children, and she thanked the Lord often for her three little ones.

'It was so easy to make friends because I had three kids and could bring them to kindergarten. When we moved house after two years we were located in a cul-de-sac off the main road, in a new area of town. It was great for Miriam, she was just six months old and could crawl about, all the doors would be open and I would sit out with the neighbours drinking chai (Turkish tea). It provided us with a perfect environment to relax together, get to know each other, and in time for me to share my life and faith with them. The kids had fun having foreigners as neigh-bours and it was here that I really started to speak Turkish.'

Unfortunately, the children didn't settle as quickly as their parents did. Michal, the eldest, found the first few months especially hard. She had travelled with her mum and dad to England and to Germany; this was her third new country. Naturally she found it tough. In the first few months after moving to Turkey, she often said, 'Mum, when do we move again?' Michal was sure that another move would be coming shortly, as that had been the pattern up until now. Both Susanne and Tilmann would do their best to reassure her that they weren't going to be moving countries again.

Susanne vividly recalls how it affected little Michal. 'For a while her childhood drawings were always in black and white; she never drew in colour.' For Susanne it was sad to see the influence moving around so much had had upon her daughter. Thankfully as time went by and they settled in Adana, Michal's drawings began having a dash of colour in them. 'The turning point came when I entered her for kindergarten. She started to draw with great bright colours then. She was nearly four years old, but she could reflect her thoughts with tremendous power. It was clear she was happier and loving kindergarten.'

Despite the happier times, Susanne and Tilmann were not where they wanted to be. They were desperate to reach the unreached. They wanted to move further east: deeper into the heartland of Islamic Turkey.

But at what cost? Susanne's words of years ago echoed in her mind: 'Everything I have is yours. Everything.'

The Work Develops

Susanne and Tilmann were in Turkey not to spend time with foreigners, but locals. While for a time language study and acclimatisation were essential, this was just a means to an end. They were here for the Turks. Their compassion for lost Muslims came from deep within them and they were ready to express it.

Their first opportunity came when a couple of key members within the Turkish-speaking church came to understand the passion that Susanne and Tilmann had for the Turkish community. The members invited them to join their church so that they could simply observe. Naturally delighted, they agreed immediately. So, over the next few months, they attended the International morning service and the Turkish afternoon service.

'As our responsibilities in both churches increased,' Susanne recalls, 'we were increasingly under greater pressure. Tilmann was often preaching in the morning while I was leading the children's work – it was becoming too much. Thankfully others noticed it too, and began to help share the burden. What was becoming obvious to all of us though was that our transition into the Turkish-speaking church was taking place. We were delighted. This was what we came for.'

A heart and passion for the Turkish people naturally led to a desire to witness to them about Christ. As Susanne openly admits, she is not a naturally pushy person when it comes to the gospel. While she will gladly talk openly about her faith, she wouldn't be the one urging people to make a decision there and then. Tilmann was of a similar disposition. Neither of them were the type to allow an opportunity pass them by, either. It was this well-rounded approach that prepared them to be great leaders of an Alpha course, designed for those wanting to explore Christianity.[3]

'There were always lots of people attending the course, between five and seven every time. We had some boys who had been through their army training. [Turkish boys are legally obliged to join the army when aged eighteen, for a maximum period of two years.] They were new believers so the course helped lay some firm foundations for their faith. Two of them are now leaders of the church.'

Seeing people come to faith brought a thrill to Susanne and Tilmann. It was what they were in Turkey to facilitate.

Until they were amongst an unreached people group in Turkey, though, they were not going to be satisfied. Their longing to be part of such a community became incessant. They knew it would involve a move, which they feared would have a negative effect on the children, partially Michal, but they trusted the Lord knew what He was doing. They awaited His prompting . . .

Darkness Personified

Susanne's Journal

'Do not be terrified; do not be afraid of them. The LORD your God, who is going before you, will fight for you . . .' Deuteronomy 1:29-30
'But when they arrest you, do not worry about what to say or how to say it. At that time you will be given what to say.' Matthew 10:19
Thank you Lord, that you carry us through.

Susanne had gone away to a women's conference, some way from home. The conference itself wasn't memorable, until she eavesdropped on a conversation between two women stood beside her. One was telling the other about their impending move to a city in south-eastern Turkey: Malatya. It was an intriguing soundbite to have overheard as she pondered her future.

When she arrived home and was unpacking her things and throwing them in the washing pile, she casually shouted through to Tilmann in the other room: 'Do you know where Malatya is?'

'Pardon?'

Walking through to the living room, still with a handful of dirty washing in her hand, she repeated her question: 'Malatya? Do you know where it is?'

Tilmann's face broke into a wry smile. He explained to Susanne why. Just a few days earlier he had been looking at the map, as he often did, and came across this eastern city, Malatya. He had thought to himself how this might be a good place for them to move to. He had already done quite a bit of research.

'He mentioned that it had a nice university, which was perfect for Tilmann because at this stage he was thinking of opening up his own business in order to start earning money; that was his goal. Not to be rich or anything, but he didn't want to depend on the government in Germany for our finances. Tilmann believed it was important to show the Turkish community that we didn't have to be dependent upon foreign money. He was keen to show that Christians can work, in a normal job, live a normal life like a normal person.

'There is a tendency, when people became believers, to try and find a job with a foreigner so that they can get lots of money from abroad. Or they will want to work for the church so that their salary was sorted.'

Obviously, Susanne and Tilmann couldn't just flee from Adana and leave the work there unsupported, but a desire for Malatya was kindled and their excitement was evident. Conversations and discussions were had with the other workers as they sought the Lord together. It soon became clear that this enthusiasm was not ill placed. The Lord was guiding not just Susanne and Tilmann, but a number of other workers too. Pausing frequently, Susanne and Tilmann would talk with the Father about what to do and when. Once again they were keen that He was to be in control of everything.

Tilmann soon opened up the Silk Road Language Consultancy with an Englishman. (Technically it was a language school, but due to government legislation it couldn't be referred to as such.) It made sense to move to a bigger city with a university where they could recruit students. 'That is when we made the move to Malatya. We spoke to other couples on our team about our interest but no one else really caught the "Malatya-bug". We were on our own.'

❀ ❀ ❀ ❀

In 2002 a reconnaissance trip to the city was suggested, agreed and arranged.

Susanne and Tilmann, without the children, went during the Sugar Feast (a feast after Ramadan) in Malatya to see what the area was like. It was not quite what they expected.

Looking back at her journal entries, Susanne remembers a horrendous first impression. Rain clouds dominated the sky wanting to dump their wetness on all who dared to venture out. Grey, dark and dismal weather inevitably produced feelings of depression. To add to the feeling of darkness, Ramadan had drawn to a close, and with the start of the Sugar Feast, everyone they saw was dressed all in black, as is their custom at that time of the festival.

It would not have been surprising if this had put them off ever returning. Maybe they would look elsewhere before making a decision. However, after just a day in Malatya, they both knew, independently and jointly, that this was the place they wanted to be.

Although their hearts were impatient to be in this strategic university city, they knew a move would not be without its difficulties. Housing was hard to come by.

Most available properties were only for sale; those that were to rent were often too expensive.

'We wanted the children to be as much a part of the move as us. This was going to be their new home so we wanted them to be happy. When we went back to see them after our visit we told them what we had seen and our possible plans. They were a little indifferent to it all and just got on with life as normal. But we planned a new trip back to the city for May so that we could find a house together, and the kids could see what they thought of the area.'

Their response was all that Susanne and Tilmann could have hoped for.

As the children stepped out of the car and lifted their heads towards the horizon, all they could see were fields and mountain ranges.

'Wow, this is green here, Mum!'

Adana was quite a dark city with hundreds of buildings surrounded by very little greenery. Malatya was a welcome change.

The city of Malatya (pronounced Mah-Laht-Yah) in southeast Turkey is located at the foot of the Anti-Taurus Mountains. It lies almost a thousand metres above sea level. Its climate and terrain is perfect for growing its number one selling export – apricots. Hot, dry summers are followed by cold, snowy winters, with the ground being well nourished by the tributaries of the Euphrates.

The area prides itself on being the leading apricot producer in the world. They are often sun-dried in family-run orchards following traditional methods. During harvest time the place is awash with them. Any view of the city, from all vantage points, shows how the small fruit dominates.

There was still one major problem. The Geskes couldn't do anything until they could find some housing. Possibilities were limited.

Hour after hour, Susanne and Tilmann would drive the suburbs of the city, hoping and praying they might find something suitable. They got restless as the sun took its toll inside their old car. Susanne was beginning to worry nothing would be found and, if that was the case, what was God saying to them?

Susanne talking to kids in Malatya.

Tilmann's diary.

Necati Aydin, Ugur Yüksel and Tilmann Geske.

Tilmann's Greek Bible.

Outside the offices.

The office where the three men were murdered.

Tilmann's office after the police search.

The sun shining on the grave.

The coffin being lowered into the ground.

The coffin in the ground with flowers.

Miriam at Tilmann's grave.

'Look, I've told you – the house is yours!'

Hope was fading of finding anything both suitable and available. This was already their second visit to the area. Renting wasn't an option – there just weren't any rental properties available, and purchasing was way out of their price range. Eighteen thousand pounds was the going rate – impossible for Tilmann and Susanne.

They returned two weeks later without the children, more desperate than ever. After some hours of searching, it was time for a much needed break. For a bit of fun, to break up the monotony of driving around housing blocks, Tilmann decided they should have some time out looking at the nice end of town. They couldn't afford the houses there, not that any were ever available, but it would be entertaining to have a look. They had already viewed a couple of houses that morning closer to the city, but they needed so much repair work done that they were unrealistically priced.

The housing blocks at this new end of town were well spaced, surrounded by mountains and lush green grass. A children's park was located just across the way. 'The kids would just love this,' Susanne thought. It was then that Tilmann spotted a little 'For Rent' sign hanging in the ground floor apartment of a building that wasn't yet fully built. They knew it would be out of their price range, as they always were, but not wanting to turn down a chance to stretch their legs, they jumped out of the car and went to have a look around.

'The house was beautiful. It would have been a perfect place to live. We were all so impressed. The rooms were spacious, leaving plenty of room for the children to play. I had a long list of things that a suitable house for us would have and I think this one met every one – it was just what we needed.'

As Susanne began to decorate each room in her mind, she remembered the small matter of their financial limitations. It was bound to be way out of their price range. They had recently checked what was available; the prospects were not looking good with a worrying lack of money in their bank balance.

They thought it was worth a call to the estate agent anyway.

'We cut straight to the point. We needed to know how much it would cost. We were expecting the landlord to tell us something like 250 lira a month. We waited with baited breath . . . 150 lira. We were amazed, and he could tell! He asked us if it was too much, we quickly replied "No, no" almost biting his hand off to have it. Trying our best to act calm amidst excitement, we asked him if we could have it and he agreed – on the payment of a deposit.'

Tilmann and Susanne dug into their pockets. Besides a bit of fluff and a paper clip, they pulled out a crumpled 20 lira note. It was all they had. They presented it to the landlord hoping against all odds that it would be enough. Unbelievably, it was. He accepted it as their house deposit, took their number down on a scrap of paper, crumpled it up and shoved it back into his pocket. He promised he would call them. They were on their way, with a house sorted. Things were looking up again. Maybe, just maybe, this was where God wanted them after all.

❁   ❁   ❁   ❁

Three days later, Susanne's nerves got the better of her. She picked up the phone and called the landlord. She had heard nothing, wondering if he had done a runner with their 20 lira – and their prospect of a house.

'Do we still have this house?' Susanne enquired.

'Yes yes! Of course!'

If he was conning them, he was certainly convincing. Anxious again, a few days later, Susanne called again.

'Are you sure it is?'

'Look, I've told you,' he replied sounding slightly agitated that she didn't seem to understand, despite being told numerous times. 'The house is yours.'

She finally felt confident – the house was theirs. Documentation was difficult for them to obtain as they were still viewed as foreigners, despite their commitment to integrating into Turkish life and society. Tilmann patiently and persistently went backwards and forwards between places to sort out the paperwork. He was the perfect partner for Susanne.

The Lord had wonderfully provided them with a house they never dreamed possible. They were excited about what He had in store for them next.

Ministry in Malatya

It was Susanne and Tilmann's wish to simply slip into the area, almost unnoticed. While in the west we may distribute press releases about the appointment of a new pastor, in the hostile environment of Turkey it is not appropriate. Unfortunately, the move didn't turn out as planned. The newspapers and the TV stations somehow got wind that a couple of Europeans had arrived, with their children in tow. They splashed photos on the front pages and the family became headline news on the local channels – announcing the arrivals of these new 'workers'. Sometime later, when the commotion and hysteria died down, Susanne sat down with a friend. 'Not exactly the quiet entrance you were hoping for!' he joked.

Tilmann was dependable and hard-working. While he kept himself to himself he ran a successful consultancy business that led to many opportunities to talk about his life and faith with clients and customers. When these opportunities came up, he loved to share Jesus with them, the best way he knew.

When Susanne and Tilmann moved into town three other couples, of three different nationalities, joined them: Turkish, British and South African. Four different agencies together with four different languages: they certainly made quite a team. Despite their differences they worked successfully together. Matthew, from South Africa was the team leader. He was a skilled organizer who found it easy to bring people together. Each month their house church would switch location between their four homes. Whichever home they found themselves in, Tilmann would always be the one helping with the music. He was a fantastic musician.

'He would often play the electric piano at home, but was too shy to play so everyone could hear. Instead he would have some headphones. I would sometimes sneak up on him and pull them out so I could hear, but he would soon plug them back in. He was a humble guy who didn't like attention.'

The team was split in two: the Turks with the Germans, the Brits with the South Africans. They would meet with their pairs each week for their Sunday service, getting together once a month so they could share updates, concerns and prayer points with each other.

Unfortunately, because of issues with their visas and other problems, Matthew the South African team leader, and his wife had to return back to their homeland during 2006, which left just the three couples. Readjusting to a team of six was not without its trials. Matthew had been a key player in the work in Malatya, so he was sorely missed. Although the shy retiring type, Tilmann rose admirably to the added responsibility that now fell his way following Matthew's departure. His consistent dependability was a real asset to the team. Tilmann's work permit had recently come to an end, so his ministry focus also had to shift. As a brilliant polyglot it only seemed right and appropriate that he should be using those gifts. Tilmann had already proven his capabilities in this arena when the occasional Turkish businessman approached him to translate German documents into Turkish or vice versa. With his theological background,

Tilmann was the man to be involved in the work of the new Turkish Study Bible, something he was gifted at and enjoyed.

'His business, Silk Road Consultancy, was involved mainly in teaching English or German, with a little bit of translation on the side too. Understanding languages came so easily to him. It was like a second nature. He couldn't do translation officially because he wasn't a Turk so he didn't have the correct documentation. You could have far better skills than the Turkish, but if your nationality is not Turkish, you can't do translation.'

This is just another way in which the Turkish government seeks to protect and promote itself. It is distinctly suspicious of outsiders, particularly those from the west. Restrictions are put in place where possible with regards to what foreigners can and cannot do within Turkish culture. Tilmann's qualification for translation came from Germany and was therefore not recognized by the Turkish authorities. Tilmann and Susanne knew a Turkish translator, who, once Tilmann had completed the translation work, could stamp his work and sign it off, in order to make it valid in the eyes of the hierarchy. This acquaintance was a real gift from God.

Tilmann always had plenty of work, despite his shyness and unwillingness to promote himself.

'He wasn't good at selling himself,' Susanne recalls. 'He would never say he was good at something, instead he would always see better qualities in someone or something else, saying, "I'm not as good as . . ." He put himself down and I would tell him, "Don't do this! You are good, you're better than most of the people here." He would never listen though.'

Although Tilmann would go around factories and offices explaining about SRC and the translation work they were able to do, it never brought in much business. If he could just get on with his translation in his office, he was happy. Having to go out and tout for business was not his forte. Most of his business came from word of mouth or repeat custom, which was an encouragement. It meant he was good at his job – even if he wasn't prepared to admit it himself.

'He translated all sorts of documents. People from the state offices would often come in and commission him to do some work in German for them. Seventy-five per cent of the world's apricot supply comes from Malatya, so he could also get some work with companies wanting translation done on their apricot products. Basically, he would teach or translate for anyone wanting it.'

Using his musical ability, Tilmann, amongst others, was involved in an Easter service at the local hotel, Altin Kayisi. While the workers couldn't issue an open invitation to all (due to security fears) they certainly did their best to get as many contacts as they knew along to the event. It was Easter Sunday and the guests were taking their seats. One of the male workers usually stood by the door welcoming people, but also keeping an eye out for special people. ('Special people' is the term used to refer to people who act or seem suspicious and could potentially cause aggravation.) However, today it wasn't possible, as they were all busy with other things, so the responsibility fell to Susanne. Not that it was a problem, she was used to doing so. As people arrived she recognized most faces.

The service was exceptional, truly revealing the message of Jesus for those who were there. Apart from three people leaving after about five minutes, everything happened as normal. No one knew that in just a few days their lives would be transformed.

Susanne's Journal

A steep and bumpy way is ahead. Probably the only way to show my love to Muslims is to be persecuted by them.

Behind the Exterior

Few people ever managed to overcome Tilmann's shyness, but when they did they discovered a true gentleman. There were four people who over time got to know this man better than anyone else. They were his wife and three children. Sat around in the living room one afternoon, they remembered their husband and father – both the good and the bad . . .

Susanne was drinking chai while snacking on a finger pastry, and Lukas was half-watching TV – chipping into the conversation every so often. The girls sat either side of their mother. Miriam, playing with her hair, occasionally threw in a comment.

Susanne, knowing him the best and longest, began.

'He was a talented sportsman,' she said before pausing, remembering him on the sportsfield. He was tall and so had a natural advantage at rowing and cycling. 'He was just like anyone else – he loved winning! At the retreats and conferences that our organization hosted for the workers, there would always be a game of football between the various sections e.g. Istanbul vs. Malatya.' Lukas's ears pricked up. He knew what was coming. 'The last conference we were at, our team from Malatya won. I played as well as Lukas, along with Tilmann – Lukas shot the . . .'

Before Susanne could finish Lukas interrupted with great excitement. 'I scored the final goal,' he exclaimed, showing no sign of inheriting his dad's timidity. Susanne walked over to the display cabinet and, with great pride, pointed out the trophy the family had won.

As any male does, whether aged ten or seventy, Lukas went on to describe every second of play leading up to and including the goal. Naturally it was an amazing goal that would seal victory.

With a proud smile, Susanne returned to her memories. 'He was so proud of his son, and the trophy he'd won for our team. Like any dad, he was thrilled with the achievement of his little lad.'

'Lukas might not have inherited his dad's humility,' Susanne said with a knowing giggle, 'but he has certainly picked up his ability to play sport. In fact,' she carried on, almost as if remembering that she had two other children, 'Michal and Miriam have too. Michal loves basketball and Miriam has recently started swimming and is doing really well.'

Despite the trophy win, Susanne and Tilmann always found the organization's conferences hard work. It wasn't that the conferences weren't any good, or of no help, but they were always such a long way away, usually taking eighteen hours to reach by bus. Like anyone else, their work had its downside.

'Don't misunderstand,' Susanne said, 'we really like seeing people and meeting with our colleagues but the conferences can be very expensive and it can be difficult to motivate yourself for them.' Susanne paused, as though she had something else to say but wasn't sure whether to say it or not. Her boldness won the day and she proceeded to speak her mind. 'We were so keen to get out of going this year we tried hard to think of a good excuse not to go.' Nonetheless the Geske family attended, creating more precious memories between both staff and family.

It was time to move on to something Susanne wouldn't get into trouble for saying and she knew it.

'He always wanted children, even when we were only just married. When they came along he would always try and play a game with us all before the kids went to bed. It was something fun that we could all do together, like a board game or turning the living room into a den for all sorts of performances, from the Blues Brothers to simply goofing around. Looking back, these family times were really special to us.'

He wasn't going to waste his musical talents either – with lessons so expensive, Tilmann taught the children music. As the oldest, Michal naturally picked up the most.

Susanne played her part too though. 'My responsibility was to get them to practice, while Tilmann told them how to do it. In the last weeks, Michal and Tilmann would sing a lot by the piano. They would try out new songs that Tilmann had written. It was lovely seeing them play and sing together.'

Then one of them piped up, remembering their dad's ability to cook the most amazing cakes without a recipe. 'Oh yes, his cakes!' Michal agreed. A look of delight across her face expressed just how good these cakes were.

Tilmann loved to serve. Come Saturday morning, he would creep out of bed, not wanting to wake Susanne. After completing his studies for that morning he would make his way into the kitchen to begin cooking a batch of bread or some pastries. The distinct aroma of warming bread would greet the family as they began to get up. The children would hurriedly jump out of bed and make their way to the kitchen. While they were more

interested in stealing a little bit of cake mixture than seeing him, Tilmann loved to have them around him.

Not only did he always clean up after himself but he
was also always the first to volunteer to help when he
could see Susanne was struggling. Whether it was a
burnt pan, or a tough bit of grease that wouldn't budge,
he didn't like to see Susanne having trouble – so he
would step in.

Tilmann was more than just a caring husband and a
fun father. He was also a spiritual man, with an ability to
teach and preach the Bible. Having studied Hebrew and
Greek at college, he kept up his study for his own bene-
fit when teaching others. 'He was a devoted prayer war-
rior. Often he would spend prolonged periods of time
praying for friends, family and neighbours. I really
admired him for that,' remembers Susanne.

Tilmann was also quite handy when it came to DIY.
'If we wanted something for the house he would draw
up the design so that he could take it to a carpenter. He
wanted, for example, to design something for the piano
to stand on but when we finally got some money he
couldn't find the guy who would build the stand any
more. Then when we found the guy, the money was
gone! Such was life. Tilmann improvised though,
building a temporary makeshift stand out of old wine
crates.'

❀   ❀   ❀   ❀

'Tilmann was quite the child when it came to festivities
like Christmas. He would make the whole thing a lot of
fun! Even when we were on our own as a family, it was
no problem to have fun, laughing and jumping around
on the sofas with the kids. He would just mess about
and the kids would absolutely love it. He wouldn't be

the kind of Dad who would buy lots of presents, he hated to do that.'

'One year when it came to the time for his birthday I told him, "I know what I will buy you, because I know you will never do it on your own . . ." and he said "What?" and I said, "A new computer." And once again he protested, saying "No, no," but I disagreed. So I bought him a new laptop. This is what I always had to do, find an excuse like a birthday. His sister gave his bike for his birthday. He bought the printer in his office as a present for me and then used it for himself! He wasn't the necklace-buying romantic sort, but I loved him all the same.'

There is one instance than illustrates Tilmann's character perfectly. 'When I close my eyes and think of Tilmann, I can picture him on our holidays. He'd be sitting quietly on the beach with the kids, enjoying the glowing sunshine, building so many sandcastles. They were structures really, rather than sandcastles. You wouldn't believe what they were able to build. It was always so precise; so perfect. And that was how Tilmann was. When he did something, even something as basic and mundane as castle building on the beach, it would be perfect: the best.'

If Susanne was trying to hide her love for Tilmann she was doing a bad job at it. It was written all over her. Her face glowed and her eyes sparkled. He had his faults, as anyone does, but he also had his tremendous qualities.

'He didn't have to be making a furore to have a good time with the kids – though sometimes he did do that. He was quite content to be sat there with them doing nothing much, chatting quietly together. It was a lovely sight.'

❀   ❀   ❀   ❀

Susanne and Tilmann weren't usually up late. Tilmann would rise fairly early to do his devotions, as he was keen to get his rest not long after the children had made their way to bed. Occasionally though, he would be tempted to stay up if a Bond film was on the TV. 'We didn't really watch a lot of films or go to the cinema – even when we were in Germany,' remembers Susanne. 'We just preferred to stay at home and read, or relax together.'

One evening just after Easter however Tilmann had sat up and watched a film. It wasn't like Tilmann to stay up and watch a film late into the evening, but this film held his interest. It portrayed the life of the Roman Emperor Nero (54 to 68 AD). Nero was a brutal man who had been brought up in an unstable household. He came to power as Emperor aged just sixteen. Ten years later, one of the most famous events of his reign took place – the fire of Rome in 64 AD. Nero was in Antium when the fire started in the Circus Maximus. The fire spread and raged furiously over Rome for nine days. When Nero returned, he started to rebuild the city, which caused some to suspect him of planning the fire in order to make room for a new city built in his honour. Nero, needing a scapegoat for the fire, chose to put the blame on the Christians. He brutally persecuted them. This persecution took on different forms: some were torn to death by dogs while others were used as torches to light Nero's gardens and parties.[4]

Tilmann was eager to discuss it with Susanne. 'We talked about persecution. We were finding it hard to imagine people being slaughtered and set alight, as in Nero's day. We knew, of course, that tragically it still happens in many parts of the world, but we just couldn't envisage it happening to us.'

Martyrdom can be defined as a 'death that is imposed because of the person's adherence to a religious faith or cause'.[5] We might ordinarily think of the physical death of someone, which in most cases is correct, but there is also a spiritual martyrdom that is commanded from believers in Christ. A death of self is required. As the author Michael Tait writes in *Live Like a Jesus Freak*, 'While we may not be called to martyr our lives, we must martyr our way of life. We must put our selfish ways to death and march to a different beat. Then the world will see Jesus.' Yes, it takes courage to be bold and passionate for Christ in our world today, but in our heart of hearts we know that He deserves nothing less.

'Dave Goodman, a missionary in Turkey over twenty-five years ago, was shot dead in the town of Adana, where we used to live – but this was the closest that we had come to real persecution. We weren't naive enough to think that it no longer happened, or that it couldn't and wouldn't ever come to us – it just seemed so distant. Tilmann wasn't fearful of anything happening, but he said we must be prepared for it should it come. You can never truly prepare for it though.'

Susanne's Journal

I think it so wonderful Lord that you had given me a clear 'yes' to be single and had prepared the way for me to go alone to the Muslim world. And then you gave me a man. I gave my life to you and you have blessed me richly and abundantly. Thank you that you have a plan. I want to be obedient and go YOUR way . . .

When I consider all the costs that Tilmann and I will face in the future I could be full of doubt. But Jesus is bigger. He has all the power and all the money in the world. He not only can but he will help us, for he has promised. Where is my faith?

Lord, take my faith, strengthen it against the temptations of Satan and let me flee to you.

Meeting with 'Seekers'

Tilmann started his day as he always did. At 5.35 a.m., his digital watch beeped, waking him. By 5.45 he was beginning his usual routine, starting the day in prayer. Nearly every day during his life as a Christian Tilmann had started his day this way. He regarded prayer and Bible reading as essentials for the day-to-day life, not just of a worker but for every Christian.

'He was totally disciplined. Wherever we would be, even on holiday, he would get up early in the morning with his Bible to read. If he didn't get a chance then he would go straightaway after breakfast to study. In all our time together as husband and wife he only missed one or two days of reading his Bible and praying. What an example and challenge he was – if only I had his discipline.'

After an hour of prayer and Bible study he would begin to make breakfast for the family. Susanne wasn't a morning person, which he quickly learnt when they got married. Being the gracious, servant-hearted man that he was, he saw it as his privilege to, each morning of their fifteen-year marriage, to wake Susanne up with a light kiss, telling her that her breakfast was ready.

Tilmann's accountant was over from Adana sorting out various bookkeeping responsibilities for the taxman, so the family enjoyed breakfast together with him. At 7.30 a.m. Michal left for school on the bus. Around an hour later, Lukas and Miriam left too.

With Edwin, the accountant about, Susanne and Tilmann neglected to kiss each other goodbye that day, to spare Edwin any feelings of embarrassment.

❀   ❀   ❀   ❀

'My cell phone rang about 10.15 a.m. and it was Tilmann. He needed some extra cash to give the accountant and asked if I could bring it down to the office as he was at his withdrawal limit. I had the amount he needed and made my way to the bakery near his office, where we had arranged to meet. He was waiting there for me and I handed him the money. I wasn't too happy that we once again had to give away more money to other people when we didn't really have enough to live on ourselves, but I trusted his judgement. I planned to apologize for my tone that evening.'

Tilmann said goodbye to his wife and headed up the stairs to his office. No doubt a little out of breath when he reached the top, he gave the money to his accountant. Taking off his knitted cardigan, he folded it neatly, placing it over the armchair, beside his umbrella. He was keen to get on with the translation work he was doing and picked up where he had left off. His door remained ajar, as workers Necati Aydin and Ugur Yüksel prepared to meet five Muslim enquirers next door.

The three of them had worked together for some time now. Though Tilmann, as ever, kept his head down, the three of them were both friends and colleagues.

❀   ❀   ❀   ❀

Necati and Ugur had been meeting various people, recent converts and seekers alike, to study the Bible for quite some time. A risky thing to do, but despite the danger they knew it brought to their own lives and their families, they counted all other things loss compared to telling people about Christ, no matter how hazardous.

Since December, the two of them had been meeting regularly with two young men, who had shown some interest. Necati had told his wife, Shemsa, of his uneasiness with a couple of the 'enquirers'. 'I'm just not sure they are seekers,' he told her. Shemsa, an optimistic character, told him not to worry too much. She wanted him to stay safe, but they knew their work was a risky one – trusting God was essential. 'Give them a Bible,' she told Necati, 'and pray they change.'

'Just tell me what you know'

It was just after 2 p.m. when Susanne's mobile phone rang. Shemsa was on the other end, sounding hysterical. She was out of breath, her voice was shaky and she was fighting back tears.

'Susanne, something must have happened,' she said hurriedly. She explained that she had received an unexpected phone call from a fellow believer in Izmir (formally Smyrna) on the west coast of Turkey, hundreds of miles away. The call was similar to the one Shemsa was now making – enquiring what was going on in Malatya, as reports were filtering through that something untoward had taken place.

Thinking the worst came naturally to Susanne at this point. She couldn't help but remember that she had tried phoning Tilmann on his mobile just before lunch but, unusually, with no success.

'The call went straight through to his voice mail, which never happened. Tilmann never switched his phone off. It was alarming. At the time, I thought the battery must have been flat; I planned to ask him that night why he had switched it off, as it was so unlike him. I began to get anxious.'

Shemsa too, had had no luck in getting through to her husband. The more the two of them tried to get through, the more frustrated and restless they became.

Susanne, Shemsa and Emma (Susanne's good friend who lived nearby) were all now busily calling friends and colleagues trying to get concrete news.

Just then, Susanne's doorbell rang. It was a neighbour from Susanne's block of flats. She was enquiring if she had heard the news of the death of a Canadian in the city, near where Tilmann worked. With Susanne being a westerner, the neighbour kindly wondered if she knew of the person concerned. Unaware of any Canadians working in Malatya, Susanne pressed for some more details. It sounded like the incident had actually taken place in the office block where Tilmann worked, a place to which Susanne rarely went. Unfortunately the news reports on Turkish TV were so frequently erroneous that watching them was worthless. Susanne was sceptical; not least because, she knew no Canadians worked there – two Americans but no Canadians.

The neighbour offered to help in any way she could, promising to return if she found out anything more.

'The phone was ringing non-stop. Everyone was doing what they could to find out any hard evidence. I was trying Tilmann's phone, but still couldn't get through. I was getting frustrated. The kids were about to get out of school and I had got no further in my investigations. I was so uptight.'

Remembering her neighbour's offer of help, Susanne called her. Optimism was rapidly dwindling. Arrangements were made for the neighbour to pick up Lukas and Miriam – twelve-year-old Michal would be making her own way on the service bus a couple of hours later, as usual.

Time went by but the reports were only marginally clearer. It was now becoming evident that something quite serious had happened at the Agbaba office block, where Tillman and his colleagues worked on the third floor. Susanne called the police hoping that they might be able to provide some facts. They were as confused as anyone.

It emerged that a couple of men had been taken to hospital. Susanne naturally pressed for more details. She failed . . . until they confirmed that a Turk named Emre, and a foreigner, wearing a cross, had been taken to hospital.

'Tilmann didn't wear a cross. He wasn't the sort of person to wear anything like that. I enquired about the nationality of the foreigner, but as ever, the police could confirm nothing. Their only evidence that the person in question was not a Turkish national was the cross around the victim's neck – in their eyes a Turk would never do that.' Hardly concrete evidence, but enough for the police to draw their conclusions. In time, Susanne and her friends would come to realize this was Ugur – their colleague.

Still unaware of Tilmann's whereabouts and unable to contact him, Susanne contacted the surrounding hospitals, desperate for any news. The phone didn't stop ringing. Friends and colleagues were calling with the same purpose – wanting confirmation of events. Then the phone rang again.

'I'm so sorry to hear the news,' said the caller. Presuming they meant the confusion of the situation Susanne accepted the caller's sympathies, but as they repeated their sympathies, Susanne stopped in her tracks. 'I'm so sorry to hear the news of the death.'

Susanne shrieked, hanging up the phone impatiently. What was going on? She raced down to the SSK, the local hospital, with Lukas, Miriam and Emma. They were greeted at reception by a group of policemen, standing around.

The police were typically unforthcoming with information. They told Susanne that they must take her immediately to the station in order to bring her family under police protection while the investigation was going on. Thankfully, the younger kids were with her. Michal was at secondary school, oblivious to the horrific events unfolding around her.

The policemen clearly knew more than they were letting on. Their phones were ringing continually. There would be a short conversation then some note scribbling, followed by scurrying around. What was it that they were hiding?

Susanne and her family sat in the police waiting-room, across the foyer. Lukas and Miriam were becoming restless.

'Mamma,' said Lukas. 'What is going on? What have they done to Papa? When can we see him?'

Susanne couldn't answer.

'I don't know, Lukas, I really don't know,' Susanne replied as tenderly as she could, stroking his face, while trying to hold back her tears. Susanne wanted to be strong for the sake of her child, even though she longed as deeply for Tilmann as much as her children did. 'Just pray that your Daddy has only been hurt,' she said.

The three of them sat in the waiting room, dazed by the commotion and uncertainty. Miriam swung her legs back and forth under the chair. Lukas was more lethargic, playing with the zip on his jacket. He wasn't enjoying this. They were being kept inside the police station like prisoners. Two dim strip lights lit up the room with dusty cobwebs and dirt doing all they could to block out the light. A low buzzing noise was coming from somewhere, irritating them all.

The mobile phone of the policeman nearest to them rang again: yet another swift conversation was had. He hung up, abruptly rose from his chair and shut the door of the waiting room. Susanne could see him through the room's window, talking quietly to the other officers. Something was wrong and she knew it. The police were withholding information from her and she wasn't prepared to sit there.

She stood up in a bout of anger. She walked out into the foyer, closing the door noisily behind her.

The policemen looked startled, certainly not expecting any confrontation. Susanne, despite her slight frame, grabbed the lead officer by his jacket.

'Tell me what you know,' she commanded. 'Tell me if my husband is dead or alive.' She saw the look on the man's face. 'Is he dead?'

The answer would break Susanne's heart.

'Yes,' replied the officer.

'Your Papa is dead'

Nothing can prepare you for that dreadful answer. In that split second, Susanne's world shattered.

Her grip on the officer relaxed. Her body was numb, her mind frozen. She stepped back, groping for the dusty door handle behind her. Lukas knew something was wrong as soon as he saw his mother's deathly pale face.

Susanne slumped into the old sofa, with her children either side. She gathered them in, like a hen would gather her chicks. Leaning into one another, they hugged together. How does a mother tell a child their father is dead? How does she explain that his life has been taken from him, seemingly, before his due time? What are children meant to do, when they see their mother trying desperately to hold back tears?

They did not know.

❀   ❀   ❀   ❀

Michal was still not with them. She remained unaware of the day's events. She hopped off the bus shortly after 5 p.m. making her way home down the dusty streets.

As she flicked off her shoes to enter the house, an army of friends and workers greeted her. The house would normally be alive with activity but this was out of the ordinary: she immediately knew that something was wrong. Her mother was still not home from sorting out some papers with the police. Despite the house being crowded, she felt alone and isolated.

Lukas and Miriam had arrived home earlier with some friends who had picked them up. The sight of her sister overwhelmed Miriam. Distraught, she ran to her bedroom, slamming the door behind her. Michal tentatively asked Lukas, 'What's going on?' He refused to answer, insisting their mother wanted to tell her. His bottom lip quivering, he too ran to his room.

Back at the station, Susanne was frustrated at the length of time the legal formalities were taking. As more and more time went by, she became increasingly anxious that Michal would find out the news from a neighbour or the TV. Despite hurrying along the police as fast as she could, they were in no rush. She had no option but to call her daughter. The day had already been a nightmare. The necessity of telling her eldest daughter of her father's murder on the phone just added to it.

So much company; so very alone

Susanne felt she was in a trance and could not hide it. According to Turkish custom, the house had filled up with visitors keen to help. It felt a little like the crowded house Jesus visited in chapter five of Luke's Gospel. When there is a death in the family, eastern hospitality is at its best, with meals provided for three consecutive days for both family and visitors.

Susanne suddenly realized that both her parents and foster parents should hear the news directly from her. The last thing she wanted was for her wider family to find out via the media. Making calls home was difficult though, so she began to write an email to them. Fighting to see through a glaze of tears she told them all she knew.

Despite the hostilities of years gone by they offered to do anything they could to help her. They were keen to fly out right away and help with the preparations for the funeral, and to take care of the children. Although Susanne was keen to see them, she wasn't sure of what was going to happen in the next few days. Her parents had never been to Malatya before and would require time to adapt culturally, in addition to the constant need of a translator. She managed to convince them that for now they should stay put. Maybe in a little while they could come out . . .

❀   ❀   ❀   ❀

The Geske home had gone from a tranquil haven to a thoroughfare for all sorts of people, each playing their roles. Some entertained the children or helped with legal procedures that were both complicated and muddled, while others made meals for the family and the crowd of guests. But amid the bustle there was a vital person missing.

Susanne sat cross-legged on the sofa, in the corner of the living room. Turkish tea was brought to her, in what seemed an unremitting flow. As she drank the tea-stained water from what looked like an oversized thimble placed on a metal saucer, tears began to roll down her cheeks. The enthusiasm her face usually carried had gone and it had been replaced by a white pallor. Motionless and speechless, Susanne looked across the room with dull eyes.

A gentle hand touched Susanne's arm, awaking her from her daze.

'Have you had any thoughts about where you would like Tilmann to be buried?' the concerned friend asked.

Susanne wiped away another tear, holding back more. She told her friend that she wasn't sure what she would like to do. While she knew that she wanted him to be buried, as opposed to cremated, she knew little else.

A brief family gathering was called. Conducted in German, the first conference of four, not five, was held. Susanne was adamant that this wasn't to be *just* her decision. Despite her children being young, inexperienced in such things, and still shell-shocked with events, Tilmann had been their father: they had the right to play a role in such important decisions.

Many deep-rooted issues regarding Turkish culture, and the family's future were at stake.

A decision was made in moments, despite its enormity. 'Dad died for Jesus in Malatya; and we are here to build a church; so we should stay and build a church.' The kids were certain of what they wanted to do – and Susanne agreed. There was no more debate to be had.

Tilmann was to be laid to rest in Turkey. The next job was to try and work out a way for his burial in Malatya to actually happen. It was not necessarily going to be easy.

Where Next?

Although the decision was made, Susanne knew all too well the ramifications of her newly acquired status. Single women, even single mothers, are not held in great esteem in Turkey. As in many countries, women without a husband can find it very difficult socially. They can be easily ostracized, particularly if they have given birth to a son. Even though the son will naturally be much younger than his mother, he is held in higher regard from birth simply because he is male. But Susanne felt she was in a slightly different position. As a foreigner, society saw her in a different light, even when Tilmann was alive. Now, after his death, they were more accepting of the idea that a foreigner might be alone, even though she had three children.

It was Wednesday evening when Susanne received a phone call. On the other end of the line was a girl claiming to have been one of Tilmann's ex-students. She had heard of his murder, and wanted to get in touch. She wanted to help.

'Nuray was the head of a human rights organization in Malatya. She said that she wanted to help me. The next day she phoned again and I told her that I wanted to bury my husband in an Armenian cemetery, the only Christian cemetery in the area. "No problem," came her reply, and she promised to sort it. We knew that for her to get permission for Tilmann to be buried there would take a minor miracle. That afternoon, the Thursday, friends gathered together in a hotel room just outside of town to have a time of prayer. It was a special time, with pastors and others from all over Turkey there. There was a real sense of unity and commitment.'

Once the prayer came to an end, a few from the human rights organization arrived at the hotel and composed a formal letter of request that would be sent to the head of the Armenian Church, detailing Susanne's request to lay her husband to rest within their grounds. 'All I had to do was put my name to it, jot in my birth date and sign it. They did the rest.'

Susanne daren't think about what she would do if the Armenian Church declined her request. There was nowhere else she could consider.

'Other than this place, there was nowhere else feasible, for all the other graveyards are Muslim. I was so happy that there was a Christian alternative to the traditional Turkish options. Without this option, I would have taken his body back to Germany.'

Her resolution to bury Tilmann in a Christian cemetery in Turkey was not met with much approval. While the Turks struggled to understand it, her German compatriots failed to see her calling to Turkey and thus, her desire to bury Tilmann in Malatya. Even the Chief of Criminal Investigation from the German Embassy did all he could to persuade her to take Tilmann back to Germany and bury him there. But she was not listening. Protest as they might, she had made up her mind. Obstacles were overcome and though pessimists said it wasn't possible ('No one has been buried there for ten years') she was not going to be deterred.

Eventually persistence paid off. A letter of permission was granted – she was given her wish. The physical labour involved in preparing the grave would have to be carried out by Susanne and her co-workers, though. Her Muslim friends would certainly take no part in the preparation of a Christian burial site.

They did their best, but the ground was dry and hard. Huge boulders littered the plot of ground that the family had been allotted. They weren't going to be able to dig a deep enough grave by themselves. The rocky ground in the Armenian cemetery that day reminded them of the parable of the sower in Matthew 13, 'When anyone hears the message about the kingdom and does not understand it, the evil one comes and snatches away what was sown in his heart.' The Bible tells us that when the gospel falls on rocky ground it has no root and lasts only a short time. The perpetrators of Tilmann's murder had certainly heard the gospel from the Christian workers in that area, but sadly it had fallen on stony ground.

God saw their need for better digging equipment and provided for them. Only God can break hearts of stone and achieve the seemingly impossible. The Geskes knew all too well that their work in Turkey was futile without the Master's enabling.

There was now just one more problem. When could Tilmann's body be released from the morgue? Endless tests and an autopsy had to be carried out. As with most things in the east, they moved at a different pace to the west . . .

Rumours and Lies

Press from around the world descended at Susanne's door; each desperate for the latest news and photos, or better still an exclusive. It had been a day since Tilmann's death, and the rumours regarding the attack were still prevalent. Reports were flying around the internet as fast as people could type them. Unfortunately, their accuracy was not as pressing an issue as their speed of delivery. Christian groups were deceived. Naturally appalled and concerned reports and prayer requests were written in haste from the Turkish church and distributed around the world.

Many who were first taken in by reports of horrendous mutilations and emasculations of the three men look back with remorse. While no one can blame them for their acceptance of such stories as truth, it's now clear that these stories were a combination of media hype and Muslim propaganda. Devoted and extreme Muslims, who were celebrating the attack, were keen that it was seen as justified and heroic. The more severe the atrocity seemed, the more laudable their acts would be.

The concern, now that the murders were less severe than was first thought, was that the world would disregard them, failing to take them as seriously as they should.

❀   ❀   ❀   ❀

Aware of their misdemeanours and exaggerations Susanne did her best to avoid the press. Her brain was not working logically and she felt unable to say anything coherent to them. In order to avoid saying something she might regret, she held back. That is, until her partners in the church, who until now had also been keen to maintain their silence, commended the opportunity it might present to speak of Christ. She perhaps wasn't going to have an hour of airtime to preach the gospel, as that isn't what the newsmen wanted, but who knows what she *might* be able to say? As the knocking on the door continued, Susanne became more and more convinced it was perhaps a wise thing to do – to take this and every opportunity, as the Bible commands.[6]

With the policeman guarding the door, and the other day-to-day chores being taken care of by others, Susanne did her best to jot some thoughts down on paper.

She tore off some scrap paper from a pile near the telephone, and started to write. The words didn't flow easily. Her heart was certain of what to say, but her brain wasn't functioning as it ought, as she was still reeling with shock. She struggled on, and eventually the page filled. Reading it back to herself, Susanne mumbled it over, as though she was reading it to the press. A funny chill went through her body as she realized what she was about to do – address the world's media. Then a second thought came to mind: could anyone hear her mumbling away? They would think she was going mad! Self-conscious and more than a little terrified of the impending attention, Susanne asked for some feedback from her church friends.

She read it aloud to them as they stood around in the kitchen. Although emotional, Susanne was holding back the tears. She knew she wouldn't be so brave when the cameras were focused on her . . .

The cameramen crowded around the back while newspaper and magazine reporters jostled for position nearer the front, holding out their digital recorders as close to Susanne as they dared. She cleared her throat and softly began to read her statement. A deathly hush fell. The only sound was the cars passing on the road outside.

> We came to this country to live a normal life, the same as the Turks came to Germany as Muslims. We wanted to come to Turkey and live here as Christians. For us this is a very hard time. I have lost my lifelong friend and the children have lost their father. But I know that Tilmann died as a martyr in the name of Jesus Christ. His blood was not in vain. For Malatya and for Turkey this is a new start. Jesus said from the cross to the people around him, 'Father, forgive them; for they know not what they do' and I want to do the same.

God had remained faithful to His word. As Jesus says in Luke 21, 'But before all this, they will lay hands on you and persecute you . . . For I will give you words and wisdom that none of your adversaries will be able to resist or contradict.'

'The Turkish people couldn't understand how anyone, let alone a vulnerable woman, could say such things and claim them to be true. It is very much an "eye for an eye" culture. Their struggle to understand led them to believe that either she didn't mean it or maybe she didn't love her husband,' one worker told us.

This is one of the difficulties with cross-culture mission work. Each applies the Word of God to their culture, but it doesn't always seem to match up with what they know. Turkish culture, for example, would hold very much to the biblical teaching of Exodus 21:24, 'An eye for an eye . . .' However, when it comes to the teachings of Jesus in Matthew 5, to 'not resist an evil person' and to 'turn to him the other [cheek] also,' they aren't so comfortable.

The Turks are not alone in this feeling of required retribution. Certainly in the first instance, Miriam, Susanne's eight-year-old daughter, felt an antagonism and resentment towards the Turkish people. Many would say it was justified, but Susanne was adamant, as she was to teach Miriam, Lukas, and Michal, that this wasn't the Christlike way to respond.

Susanne knew that Christ himself had suffered much worse. 'The Bible describes how He grew up before God – a scrawny seedling, a scrubby plant in a parched field. There was nothing attractive about him, nothing to cause us to take a second look. He was looked down on and passed over, a man who suffered, who knew pain firsthand. One look at him and people turned away. We looked down on him, thought he was scum. But the fact is, it was *our* pains he carried – *our* disfigurements, all the things wrong with us. We thought he brought it on himself, that God was punishing him for his own failures. But it was our sins that did that to him, that ripped and tore and crushed him – *our sins*! He took the punishment, and that made us whole. Through his bruises we get healed. We're all like sheep that've wandered off and got lost. We've all done our own thing, gone our own way. And GOD has piled all our sins, everything we've done wrong, on him.'

Not just that, but 'He was beaten, he was tortured . . . Like a lamb taken to be slaughtered . . . Justice miscarried, and he was led off – and did anyone really know what was happening? He died without a thought for his own welfare, beaten bloody for the sins of my people. Even though he'd never hurt a soul or said one word that wasn't true.'

He was totally sinless. And yet, despite the miscarriage of justice, the betrayal of friends, the loneliness and brutality of all of this, we're told – 'he didn't say a word . . . like a sheep being sheared, he took it all in silence.'[7]

Tilmann and Susanne had taught their children this example from an early age, as many Christian families do. They were being tested now. The call to resist retribution was made – and Susanne's response would be scrutinized. How the local Turks reacted would play a key part in Susanne's future there.

The Facts

Susanne and Tilmann had never been frequent TV watchers. They didn't have the time. After finishing off jobs around the house and getting the kids to bed, there wasn't much time left for the TV. There was one programme they liked to catch if they could though: *CSI Miami*, an American drama about a team of forensic scientists.

'We'd only started watching it about six months earlier, but we both really enjoyed it,' she remembers with a fond glow on her face. 'Looking back now, it's amazing how it helped me. I'm so grateful that we began tuning in to it . . .'

Susanne couldn't face being the one to formally identify Tilmann's body. Instead she left that to a couple of friends who kindly stepped in for her.

She found herself alone in the office of the mortuary. As one does at times like this, Susanne allowed her eyes to wander around the room in a daze. There were dirty coffee cups sitting on the desk, and a crumby plate. She was still shell-shocked, hurting, and feeling almost completely alone.

She jigged a few papers, pulling and nudging them away from under the coffee cup so she could see them better. A brown file sat near the top, and had upon it, in big letters: 'Autopsy Report'. Susanne took a closer look. No one except the police had seen the report, which hadn't helped in dampening the rumours and theories that were spreading like wild fire.

Susanne was eager to know the truth, in order to correct the falsities. She tentatively picked up the file and opened it: before her very eyes Tilmann's autopsy report glared back.

'Had it not been for watching *CSI* in those previous months, I wouldn't have had a clue what the terminology I was reading meant,' Susanne looks back, with a wry smile. She would never have thought it, but the Lord knew what He was doing when He got them interested in watching that particular programme. She was about to be the only civilian to see Tilmann's report – her heart was broken yet profoundly grateful.

The report confirmed that Tilmann had been tortured.[8] As a result, there were deep blue, almost black, bruises strewn over his torso and thighs. His attackers had been brutal and relentless. Kicked and punched, Tilmann and his two colleagues were then tied up by their hands and feet to the chairs that sat in the office. The coroner had reasoned that it was then, while tied to the chair, that Tilmann was stabbed. While first reports told of hundreds of stab wounds, the reality, according to the papers in front of her, was that Tilmann was stabbed fifteen times in his chest and abdomen.

Susanne fought back her sobs. Her stomach had turned several times as she read through the papers, but as the notes she read came to the cause of death, she could hold back her grief no longer. Tears streamed down her face once more.

The documents confirmed that Tilmann's body had suffered horrific wounds both in and on his body. He died, it is presumed, shortly after having his throat cut.[9]

One can only imagine what was going through Susanne's mind as she closed up the file and arranged the papers back into the scattered mess she had found them. Susanne finds it hard to remember, 'I was numb. I didn't know what to think, where to turn or what to do. Although I was aware of support from my organization and fellow workers, even neighbours from my apartment block, I still felt a sense of unimaginable isolation. My best friend, partner, lover, husband and father of my children had been ripped from me.'

'Ignorance is bliss', so says the common phrase, but Susanne could not endorse that in her case. She was thankful to know the facts, when so much hearsay was being used in its place. Although nothing right now would or could compensate for the loss of Tilmann, some reliable information regarding the situation was mildly comforting.

Susanne's Journal

'I urge you . . . to offer your bodies as living sacrifices, holy and pleasing to God' (Rom. 12:1).

I need to be a sacrifice for God and follow Him. Romans 12 says,

> *'Do not repay anyone evil for evil. Be careful to do what is right in the eyes of everybody. If it is possible, as far as it depends on you, live at peace with everyone. Do not take revenge, my friends, but leave room for God's wrath, for it is written: "It is mine to avenge; I will repay," says the Lord.*

On the contrary:

"If your enemy is hungry, feed him; if he is thirsty, give him something to drink.

In doing this, you will heap burning coals on his head." Do not be overcome by evil, but overcome evil with good.'

But this is so, so difficult. It's something one must do, but one thing which I know I can never succeed in - but I know 'I can do everything through him who gives me strength' (Phil. 4:13).

The Funeral

The morning of the funeral was like any other April day in Turkey. The clouds were heavy, although no rain had started to fall just yet. They were showing potential however, and soon enough spots of rain were felt by those milling around outside. Inside the house, Susanne and the children were getting ready for the car to pick them up and take them to the cemetery.

'It was a surreal morning. I wasn't quite sure what to do. We had not been in a position like this before.'

Getting a balance between mourning and celebrating Tilmann's life was paramount for the family. They were going to miss him so much. They knew there was nothing they could do to bring him back. Their hearts would break daily as they longed to have him back: to talk to him; touch him; hug him and be hugged by him. While these natural feelings were present, they were also keen to honour God in their mourning. Susanne and the children (as far as their understanding let them) knew that Tilmann's death was no accident. God had not made a mistake; He had not taken His 'eye off the ball'. He was still very much upon His heavenly throne. Susanne was resolute that this should be conveyed.

Susanne knew the importance of allowing Scripture to saturate her mind and heart at this time. A verse from

Isaiah 61 came to her mind. 'For I, the LORD, love justice; I hate robbery and iniquity. In my faithfulness I will reward them . . .' Susanne knew the Lord was on her side. He hates robbery, and for sure Tilmann's life had been stolen from him. Despite the regrets of the past, and the fear and anxiety for the future, if God was for Susanne and her family, who could oppose them and destroy them?

Tilmann's funeral would allow them to express their enormous grief but Susanne also wanted it to be an occasion to give glory and praise to God. Susanne's love, her husband, had been taken from her, but God had never left her.[10]

Most if not all of the preparations for the funeral had been taken charge of by a firm in Antalya. They had frequently worked with the German Embassy before when German nationals had died in Turkey. With a solid reputation preceding them, Susanne was more than happy to let the firm take over on this occasion too. Susanne was baffled as to how this firm came into possession of her phone number – she certainly hadn't ever contacted them.

'They just arrived and said, "We will help with all the paperwork and you don't have to pay for it." I didn't know what to say, I was shocked.' When she found out just how much it would have cost her, Susanne's shock grew. They weren't cheap.

'I don't know why they came to help but I'm so glad they did. They came and took over everything, all the things like making the coffin. Everything they did was perfect, from the flowers to bringing in a machine to dig the hole for the grave. It was so nicely done. They really took over. We had no clue what we needed, but they knew.'

It was such a comfort for Susanne to know that she could trust someone to take care of the practicalities of the day. The Lord had answered prayer, providing 'immeasurably more'[11] than the basic needs of adequate digging equipment. She was still in a state of shock and struggling to come to terms with the horrific loss of her husband. This was one comfort.

At this stage Susanne still hadn't got permission for Tilmann to be buried in the Armenian cemetery. There were conflicting messages coming to her as to whether this would be possible or not. It was an anxious wait.

'On one hand plans were going forward for the funeral, while on the other hand we still didn't have permission from the governor. Then the guy from the Embassy phoned the ambassador and he in turn phoned the Foreign Affairs Minister. A whole chain of phone calls had to be made before we could move forward. Eventually the governor of Malatya was contacted and it was all passed. "Do whatever they want," he said generously. And it was an order of the highest level. No one could stop us now. It was full steam ahead.'

The firm were also keen to help Susanne and the family with the potential media scrum that would want to attend the funeral. 'I don't want any media in the cemetery' Susanne stated. She knew that it would be taken care of. While Susanne didn't want to miss an opportunity for spreading the good news of Christ, she was also a mother with others to think about. She needed to consider the needs of her children. They needed their space too, as did she. Each of them had responded to the death of their father in their own unique way. While Miriam, the youngest, was struggling to come to terms with it all, Lukas wanted to be the man of the house. He wanted to rise to the challenge of being the new 'man'.

'Mum?' he asked one morning, 'How do we earn money? Where do you get money to buy our food and pay our rent?'

Knowing that Tilmann usually looked after the paying of bills and the like, Lukas was concerned how they would cope.

'Don't be concerned,' replied Susanne with some amount of compassion and a degree of pride, knowing that her son was worrying about their well-being. 'We will earn money, it will be OK,' she reassured him.

Lukas couldn't understand how this would work though. Susanne was now a single mum with responsibilities in the home. She couldn't work too, could she? Certainly Turkish culture wouldn't see it as a favourable option.

'Don't be worried,' she said, bringing Lukas into her side for a hug. 'The Lord will look after us,' she added with total confidence and certainty. He had looked after them thus far, with Tilmann around: Susanne was prepared to trust Him to be with them now, even though the breadwinner was gone. Lukas was making his mother happy – he was being so sweet and considerate. But she was worried he was trying to do too much. 'Please, don't try to be Dad, just be yourself; try to be yourself.'

❀   ❀   ❀   ❀

At 3 p.m. Susanne and family were expecting to be able to receive the body of Tilmann, which would travel in front of them as they drove to the cemetery. The time came and went, and there was still no sign of Tilmann's coffin. While things often move slowly in the east, this was something that they were expecting to be punctual.

After all, the service was going out live on TV, they could hardly keep the media hanging around. New arrival times for the delivery were given, but passed just as soon as they arrived. Eventually, the coffin arrived in a black hearse just before 4 o'clock.

Later on, Susanne learned why it had taken so long for the authorities to release the body to be brought to her for burial. They had to wait for special troop police to deal with the hordes of people that had gathered, wanting to see the hearse pass by, in order to pay their respects. A touching act of kindness from a city that had conceded that one of their own had taken the life of a foreign guest.

The car for Susanne and the children arrived outside the flat too. It was black with shiny wheels and polished windows. Friends, neighbours, police and security officials swarmed like bees around a honey pot. Each was playing their part in a surreal day. For some, their part was protection, and others were just intrigued neighbours confused by the whole event – uncertain of who to believe: the press, the hearsay or the foreigners that they only knew to say 'Hi' to.

A commotion began just inside the door of Susanne's home signalling they were about to make their way out of the home and into the awaiting car. Like celebrities being escorted to their car from a hotel, Susanne, two of her friends and the children were whisked into the car.

No one was sure of the reception that would greet the family when they arrived at the Armenian cemetery. Certainly no one expected the great commotion that confronted them as they pulled up at the entrance. Journalists, cameramen and photographers jostled for position, desperate to get a comment or a photo. National interest was high in this 'foreigner' who had offered forgiveness to the perpetrators of this atrocious murder; a foreigner that failed to show resentment or malice toward the country where her husband had been killed.

Some confusion had arisen as to the time of the funeral. Many had thought it was to take place shortly after lunch, so they had been hanging around since then. The delay had not caused them to drift away. It took extra time for the family to get through the press.

This was not the usual place to start laughing but Susanne and the children couldn't help themselves. The situation was overwhelming. Cameras were being thrust into their faces through the tinted windows whilst the flashes were illuminating their faces.

'I had to tell the children "Don't laugh, don't laugh, don't look out of the windows." They felt like celebrities. We were surrounded by paparazzi.'

Two of Susanne's friends had accompanied them in the car to look after the children when it came to getting out. They had guessed that there would be some media interest but nothing like this. Before the funeral they had devised a system, involving Susanne's two friends, which saw each one of them taking care of the children, to ensure they weren't grabbed or jostled on their arrival.

The police stepped in. An area was set up for the media, not allowing them to enter the funeral premises. Despite the national interest, Susanne, the three children and the guests had to be protected. They deserved the opportunity to grieve, without the media in their face.

The media scrum dispersed, making their way over to a house that overlooked the cemetery. Just a few million Turkish lira would secure entrance to the occupant's balcony, which provided a perfect viewpoint to film the whole event. All of the stations would be covering it extensively in their news bulletins; one would be exclusively broadcasting the whole ceremony on their channel.

Six Christian friends and co-workers of Tilmann's slowly carried the coffin from the car. A large mob followed in procession all around them, as the coffin was gently laid next to the grave. The service could finally begin, with Susanne surrounded by her friends and colleagues. She stood, with her arms resting down the front of Lukas and Miriam, holding them close. Michal stood alongside them, one arm fastened around her mother's waist.

Officials from Germany had graciously made their way over from Ankara in order that they might show their solidarity with the Geskes. Turkish officials also joined the entourage.

Large wreaths, about four feet in diameter, had been placed on stands either side and at the head of the grave, given by various groups, both Christian and secular.

Clouds gathered in the afternoon sky. Nahamia, a leader of a Turkish church, started the service.

'Tilmann's body lies before us,' he began, 'and we miss him immensely. This is only natural. But something from Tilmann is missing. Something is not being buried with his body today. His soul. His soul is not in the coffin.'

Nahamia took off his jacket, keen to illustrate the point. Putting the navy blue coat on the coffin, he explained again that Tilmann had gone. He had been called home. But before he went he had passed his 'jacket' onto the Christians in Turkey and he needed them to 'please put it somewhere'. There was a job still to be done, a mandate for the local Christians to pick up the baton. They needed to remember Tilmann, and the reason he was in Turkey –

they needed to continue the work he had been called to –
to preach Christ to all those who questioned his reason for
such a hope.[12]

Where am I?

Would you like to know where I am?
I am at home in my Father's house, in the mansions prepared for me here.
I am where I want to be – no longer on the stormy sea,
   – but in God's safe, quiet harbour.
My sowing time is done, and I am reaping;
   – my joy is as the joy of harvest.

Would you like to know how it is with me?
I am perfect in holiness.
Grace is swallowed up in glory.

Would you like to know what I am doing?
I see God, not as through a glass darkly, but face to face.
I am engaged in the sweet enjoyment of my precious
   Redeemer.
I am singing hallelujahs to Him who sits upon the throne,
   – and I am constantly praising Him.

Would you know what blessed company I keep?
It is better than the best on earth.
Here are the holy angels and the spirits of just men made
perfect . . .
I am with many of my old acquaintances with whom I
   worked
   – and prayed, and who have come here before me.

Lastly, do you know how long this will continue?
It is a dawn that never fades!
After millions and millions of ages, it will be as fresh as
it is now.
Therefore, weep not for me![13]

❀   ❀   ❀   ❀

Despite the German connections, this was very much a
Turkish funeral. The oldest believer in Turkey was present, subject to Turkish custom he was allowed to speak
if he so desired. He did just that. It wasn't planned, but
again he shared from God's Word, urging the believers
to follow the life of sacrifice for Christ that Tilmann had
demonstrated. He passionately paced up and down,
raising his hands and pointing to the skies. This man
was a godly brother with a timely message. Though not
in the service plan, no one complained.

When he had finished, he closed his worn Turkish
Bible and handed back to Nahamia.

Susanne knew what was coming next and braced herself for the emotion it would bring. She, with Michal and
Liz, a close friend of the family, were going to sing two
songs that Tilmann had written in the last year of his life.
As a talented musician, Tilmann was able to write
music, but for a long time he hadn't really given it a try.
He had only finished two compositions but Susanne was
going to sing one of them. Braving the tears that would
no doubt come, the three of them, accompanied by a guitar, began to sing.

The cameras were still rolling from the balcony above,
broadcasting the cries of Tilmann's heart sung by his
widow, child and friend. Tears were accompanied by a
few spots of rain and before long the dark, grey clouds
above would empty themselves upon the crowd below,

camouflaging their tears with the rain. It was as if God's very creation was groaning at the seeming injustice.

> For all creation is waiting eagerly for that future day when God will reveal who his children really are. Against its will, all creation was subjected to God's curse. But with eager hope, the creation looks forward to the day when it will join God's children in glorious freedom from death and decay. For we know that all creation has been groaning as in the pains of childbirth right up to the present time.[14]

Umbrellas went up over the mourners. The singers persevered despite soggy music sheets. An umbrella held behind the trio offered little protection from the elements. As the songs drew to a close the crowd shuffled a little, keeping as warm and comfortable as they could.

Strangely, the clouds were growing darker, but the rain had, for now, come to a halt. Umbrellas began to go down, the crowd keeping them close in case of another downpour. Once the rustling had quietened down, Muratt, a good friend of Tilmann's moved to the graveside and began to speak.

> My beloved friend and brother Tilmann . . . I knew him for nearly seven years. He was a very precious friend and for us his death is a very big loss. He always was friendly, calm, and tender-hearted. He was a man who loved all people; he was full of love. His love for Turkey and the Turks was so evident and desirable.

Murat unfolded the second half of his notes before carrying on.

> Tilmann was a role model. He sang songs with his guitar for the Lord. For Turkey and the Turkish people it's a

> big loss but we know that he died for Jesus as a martyr
> and he is now with his Lord and Saviour. He died
> because he loved Jesus and the people.

Turkey, its media, politicians and people may not have
liked to admit it, but they were witnessing the funeral of
a man who had given his life to two things: firstly Jesus
Christ, his Saviour. And, because of that unwavering,
dogged commitment to Him, Tilmann had given his life
seeking to reach the people he loved: the Turks.

❋   ❋   ❋   ❋

The time had come for Tilmann's body to be buried. As
ropes were put in place to aid the lowering of the body,
Susanne and the children edged forward to the side of
the grave. Squeezing Miriam's hand, Susanne began to
cry. This was her final goodbye. Surrounded by friends,
but missing the one man who meant most to her. Never
had she thought, as she stood in front of her bed so
many years ago, declaring 'everything' as the Lord's,
that it would include her beloved husband. Her vow
before her heavenly Father that day now harshly confronted Susanne's tear-stained face, as she focused upon
the scene unfolding before her eyes, all the while clinging to the reality that *nothing* can ever separate those
who are in Christ from the loving care and protection of
almighty God.[15]

Marked with a simple cross, the coffin was lowered
into the grey earth below. The sky was heavy and the air
around them cold. Despite the certain hope of a wonderful reunion on the other side of Christ's return,
Susanne refused to hold the emotion in any longer. As
she tossed a single red carnation on to Tilmann's coffin,
she let out a cry of anguish. Looking up to the skies, she

allowed the tears to descend. There were too many to hold back. Handfuls of earth were thrown in as the coffin reached its final resting point. This was the end.

A Ray of Light

At a time like this where can one go? You can hardly blame the questioners, the doubters, and the cynics. Where is God at a time like this? The promise Susanne knew, despite the all-encompassing grief of this time, was that Jesus was now exactly where He had been the day before, and the day of Tilmann's murder: 'sat at the right hand of the Father.'[16] Susanne was still confident she could protect her heart from being troubled. She was determined to trust in God, and her Saviour Jesus Christ. Though Tilmann was absent from this earth, he was present with the Lord. Susanne knew that Jesus was God, and would not lie when He told his disciples that He was going on ahead of them to prepare a place for them . . . so that they also could be where He was.[17]

With the clouds encroaching on the afternoon sky, Susanne turned her face once more toward the grave. Lukas and Miriam were still huddling around their dear mother, longing for some comfort. Her face was red and blotchy, and she was still crying. From behind dense, blackened clouds came a ray of sunlight. It broke through with a triumph and splendour not seen on days like these. Its beam shone directly and unmistakably upon the grave and those gathered around it.

I lift up my eyes to the hills—
　　where does my help come from?
My help comes from the LORD,
　　the Maker of heaven and earth.

He will not let your foot slip—
　　he who watches over you will not slumber;
indeed, he who watches over Israel
　　will neither slumber nor sleep.

The LORD watches over you—
　　the LORD is your shade at your right hand;
the sun will not harm you by day,
　　nor the moon by night.

The LORD will keep you from all harm—
　　he will watch over your life;
the LORD will watch over your coming and going
　　both now and forevermore (Ps. 121).

Unaccompanied and unscripted, friends started to sing,
led by Michal.

　　Father God, I wonder how I managed to exist
　　Without the knowledge of Your parenthood and Your
　　loving care
　　But now I am Your son, I am adopted in Your family
　　And I can never be alone
　　'Cause Father God, You're there beside me
　　I will sing Your praises
　　I will sing Your praises
　　I will sing Your praises
　　Forever more

I will sing Your praises
I will sing Your praises
I will sing Your praises
Forever more.[18]

Michal and her brother and sister were now fatherless in the world's eyes, but some years ago, when they had responded to Christ's death on the cross for them, they had gained a Father like no other. How they would manage to exist without the parenthood of their quirky, loving father they did not know yet. But they had their Father God. As the song says – adopted into His family, they could never be alone.

After singing another couple of songs and Turkish hymns, Michal led the crowd in an emotional and unforgettable rendition of 'Oh, when the saints go marching in'. With tears pouring down the faces of nearly all who were gathered, smiles and cries of joy also accompanied them. Tilmann had gone, but he had gone to be with his Saviour.

We are trav'ling in the footsteps
Of those who've gone before
And we'll all be reunited
On a new and sunlit shore

Oh, when the saints go marching in
Oh, when the saints go marching in
Lord, how I want to be in that number
When the saints go marching in

And when the sun refuse to shine
And when the sun refuse to shine
Lord, how I want to be in that number
When the sun refuse to shine

And when the moon turns red with blood
And when the moon turns red with blood
Lord, how I want to be in that number
When the moon turns red with blood

Oh, when the trumpet sounds its call
Oh, when the trumpet sounds its call
Lord, how I want to be in that number
When the trumpet sounds its call

Some say this world of trouble
Is the only one we need
But I'm waiting for that morning
When the new world is revealed.[19]

Christians have something to sing about, even in the worst of times, as Susanne and family could vouch. Though they knew not what the days ahead would hold, and daren't consider beyond the days, they held God to His promise that He would be with them; He would comfort them.

Singing the praises of our Almighty Father may come as second nature when things are going well. How easy it can be to sing in times of great joy and excitement. But when the tough times come, and the world isn't how we want it, can we sing 'Blessed be the name of the Lord'? When we sing 'On the road marked with suffering' and 'there's pain in the offering' will our hearts still sing 'Blessed be Your name'?[20] Susanne and her children can humbly say, 'We did.'

When your world falls apart, what do you do? Susanne had no answer but to carry on the task that she and Tilmann had been doing before his murder. For their direction in life, they had trusted in God. When financial matters arose, they depended on the Lord.

When worries and concerns knocked at the door of their minds, they would bring them before God in prayer. Though Tilmann was gone, Susanne's Lord was as trustworthy and as faithful as before – His grace would be sufficient.[21] Could she continue to trust in a God who had permitted this dreadful robbery of life to take place? The world was witnessing a woman declaring 'Yes'.

> There is an endless song
> Echoes in my soul
> I hear the music ring
> And though the storms may come
> I am holding on
> To the rock I cling
>
> How can I keep from singing Your praise
> How can I ever say enough
> How amazing is Your love
> How can I keep from shouting Your name
> I know I am loved by the King
> And it makes my heart want to sing
>
> I will lift my eyes
> In the darkest night
> For I know my Saviour lives
> And I will walk with You
> Knowing You'll see me through
> And sing the songs You give
>
> I can sing in the troubled times
> Sing when I win
> I can sing when I lose my step
> And fall down again
> I can sing 'cause You pick me up
> Sing 'cause You're there

I can sing 'cause You hear me, Lord
When I call to You in prayer
I can sing with my last breath
Sing for I know
That I'll sing with the angels
And the saints around the throne.[22]

One week later, across the other side of the country in Izmir, a remembrance service was held for the three men. In an old crowded church, a brave twelve-year-old girl stepped forward to the microphone. That girl was Michal. Slightly shaking with nerves, she unfolded her script.

> I believe my father had, in the last months of his life, some feelings that something would happen. Something terrible. Something unexpected. My dad would remind us frequently in our family's daily worship together that Jesus is coming back soon and we need to be ready. Jesus will come soon. It's only a short time away.

Michy, as she was affectionately known by those closer to her, paused for breath to wipe a stray tear seeping out from under her eye. She was resolute she would not cry, but as she looked down again at the statement in front of her, she could not hold back. Another tear threatened, and then another. Before long, she was weeping. Her mum squeezed her close in a side-on hug as Michy resumed reading her tribute.

> My father really lived close to the Lord and he died for the Lord. He always lived to please the Lord. He had great musical abilities and wanted to put this into new worship songs so he wrote two songs and we want to

show you one of these so that you also may listen and praise God with these new songs.

All three of them, Necati, Ugur and Papa, are now in a far better place.

An understanding of what she was saying dawned upon her. It was true, from the heart, and because of that, it hurt so much. Her face turned red, and her chin began to quiver. Tears were now being replaced with sobs. She was determined to finish. She had just one more sentence to go.

They have sown, and the time has come when we must reap.

In one sentence, Michy had summed up her father's passion that she had also inherited. Michy and her daddy had been close. How she longed to have him back, just one more day; to have just one more hug with him; just one more crazy game in the living room.

Worldwide Response

From politicians to diplomats, religious leaders to area officials, the death of Tilmann and his two colleagues brought responses from all over the world.

While some senior officials waited a little longer to comment, allowing reports to be confirmed, Eddie Lyle, CEO of Open Doors UK, was quick to condemn the murders.

> This tragic incident is the latest example of a worsening trend of persecution against Christians in Turkey that we cannot ignore any longer. Christians in Turkey are constantly under attack. They are crying out for help and they need our prayers to strengthen them. We can, and must, answer that call. We must ask ourselves the question, "What is it that causes young men to act with such violence and hate towards innocent people, living simply and going about their daily work?"
>
> It is vital that the circumstances which generated such heinous crimes are not allowed to exist, so that Christians in all countries can freely witness to their faith and worship without the spectre of persecution hanging over them.

A similar feeling of abhorrence came from leaders throughout Europe. With the possibility of Turkey joining the European Union, at this stage an act like this, whether religious or nationalistic, was especially difficult.

The Turkish government wanted to be seen to do the right thing, given their possible political future within Europe. Sceptics were beginning to question this future as this wasn't the first murder of a Christian in their country. Fifteen months earlier, Father Andrea Santoro, a Catholic priest, was shot from behind by a sixteen year old in Trabzon, in a religious attack 'committed in the name of Allah . . . a gift to the state and the nation'.[23] An outspoken Armenian journalist, who had openly criticized Turkey, also had his life taken from him at the hands of Turkish nationals wishing to protect their country's profile. The pressure upon the government was being maximized.

Many Eastern countries are like this. In Thailand, for example, there is a strong and widespread understanding that 'to be Thai is to be Buddhist'. Similarly in Turkey, to be Turkish is to be Muslim. While not all nationals would subscribe as thoroughly to Islam as some would like, the consensus would be to acknowledge Islam to some degree, even if minor. Therefore foreign workers of a different religion are severely frowned upon at the very least. It's unsurprising that there was confusion as to what had motivated the murders of Tilmann, Necati and Ugur. Some proud nationals claimed it as a victory for Turkey and its future. Others, Islamic zealots, were keen to claim it on behalf of Allah.

As time went by the difficulty in distinguishing between religion and nationalism became all the more obvious. With all five young assailants now in Turkish custody, the national press learned that they had each admitted during initial interrogations that they were motivated by both 'nationalist and religious feelings'. 'We did this for our country,' an identical note in the pockets of all five young men read. 'They [the Christians] are attacking our religion.'

While the politicians may argue over the motivation of the attacks, and seek to defend their particular areas of interest, it was becoming clear as the dust settled that Tilmann and his two co-workers had been martyred for Christ. They knew the dangers of working in Turkey but it had not deterred their efforts.

The attack was the first known martyrdom of Turkish converts from Islam since the founding of the Turkish Republic in 1923, but it was the third tragic incident targeting Christians in Turkey in the past year or so to spark major international media coverage.[24]

Naturally, Susanne needed the support of her organization and they didn't disappoint. As soon as the news was confirmed that Tilmann's life had been taken from him, Ed, the organization's Turkish Director, and his wife Kathy flew in on the first flight available.

'I didn't want to be alone. I felt isolated and abandoned – not because friends and colleagues weren't looking after me, because they were tremendously, but because I was missing Tilmann.'

The organization ensured Susanne wasn't left alone. In time she would need her space, as life began anew as a single parent, but that time was not now. She needed comfort, love and support. The organization was more than happy to ensure she had these things.

In due time Susanne's foster parents made the journey from Germany to Malatya. A mixture of emotions flooded their minds as they tried their best to prepare themselves for their first encounter with their widowed daughter, and fatherless grandchildren. Susanne recalls their time together . . .

'It was a few weeks later, in the middle of May, that they came to see us. They were here to celebrate my birthday with me. Amazingly, a new flight had just opened up allowing you to fly from Germany to Malatya directly. Their visit, their first to Malatya, helped them see what it was really like. My foster parents were able to in turn take back first-hand news and experiences of Malatya, which allowed more distant relatives and friends get a real picture of what was going on.'

Not all were so sure that Susanne was doing the right thing. She had made up her mind that she would stay in Malatya. The three kids wanted to stay there, as did she, but many thought she would pack her bags immediately and head home, at least for some time.

In a phone call home a few days later, Susanne's birth mother made her feelings clear. She wanted her to come home.

'You're crazy for wanting to stay,' she cried down the phone line. Susanne wasn't interested. She had made up her mind. She wasn't going anywhere; she had come to Malatya to do a task, a task that had not yet been completed.

'Our phone call came to an abrupt end. I wasn't prepared to be told what to do by my mother. She didn't understand the situation: my desires, my work in Malatya.'

With an unceremonious lack of dignity Susanne slammed the receiver down. Her mother just wasn't getting that she was not coming home.

Martin Luther King once said that, 'If a man has not discovered something he will die for, he is not fit to live.'[25] Tilmann, Necati and Ugur had certainly, by the grace of God, discovered something that they were willing to die for. And God saw fit that they could and would die for its cause. As they did so, the world sat up and took notice, while heaven welcomed home three faithful servants who received the crown of life, martyrs for their Saviour.

> The Spirit of the Sovereign LORD is on me,
>> because the LORD has anointed me
>> to preach good news to the poor.
>> He has sent me . . . to comfort all who mourn, and
>>> to provide for those who grieve in Zion—
>> to bestow on them a crown of beauty
>> instead of ashes,
>> the oil of gladness
>> instead of mourning,
>> and a garment of praise
>> instead of a spirit of despair.
>> They will be called oaks of righteousness,
>> a planting of the LORD
>> for the display of his splendour.

> They will rebuild the ancient ruins
>> and restore the places long devastated;
>> they will renew the ruined cities
>> that have been devastated for generations.

> Instead of their shame
>> my people will receive a double portion . . .
>> and so they will inherit a double portion in their land,
>> and everlasting joy will be theirs. (Is. 61:1–7)

Justice and Forgiveness

How does one react to the perpetrators of such a vile act? Our heads call for justice while our hearts beg for revenge. While justice is right and fair, what should a Christian do? Are we to accept and tolerate sin, for we know the sinful world in which we live, or do we stand against it and seek for it to be brought to trial?

Susanne had made a bold statement when talking to the world's media, offering heartfelt and unreserved forgiveness to the attackers. But Miriam wanted to go a step further.

'Mum?' she asked innocently, 'When do we go to these men?' Susanne did understand. 'You know, the men . . .' Miriam replied, waving her hands as though trying to recall the name. Her mum was good, but not telepathic. Eventually Miriam's memory returned. 'The guys who killed Papa, Necati and Ugur.'

Susanne wondered why Miriam wanted to go to see them. She had to explain her motives. 'We need to go and see the men, then we can give them a Bible and then they will get to know the Lord. When they die, they can say sorry to Dad and Necati and Ugur in heaven.'

Her daughter's faith and courage filled Susanne with awe. She hadn't previously seen what a deep desire for the Lord her younger daughter possessed.

'She was an inspiration to me,' Susanne said later on. She contemplated again for a moment just what a special gift her children were to her. So often time had rushed by and she had failed to appreciate them just as much as she should. 'If I could meet these men in prison, I would try and give them a New Testament and say "I forgive you with all of my heart but there is Someone you need forgiveness from as well, the Lord Jesus. So if you feel anything in your heart to read the Bible and make that commitment, please, please do so."'[26]

'While I can offer my forgiveness, there is One greater whom they will need to account to. I would love them to be right with Him. He is the One they have sinned against. My confidence comes from the fact that He is a just God. He will bring justice even if we never see it on this earth. The Bible teaches that while wicked men seem to prosper, their ways are thwarted and lead to destruction. Only because of that truth and confidence in God can I face the perpetrators and offer them forgiveness.'

As Shemsa Aydin said at a women's conference shortly after the funeral of her husband Necati

> Forgiveness sets us free, and it is a powerful resolution of love against unjust pain. Love does not keep an account of wrong. To forgive is a decision and a gift. If we want to protect our hearts from the knives of the murderers we have to choose to forgive. Not to forgive, not to leave judgement to God, is the same as disregarding His authority. The Lord unconditionally forgave us with His own holy and priceless blood, and so we also ought to forgive others.

> Do not fret because of evil men
>   or be envious of those who do wrong;

for like the grass they will soon wither,
like green plants they will soon die away.

Trust in the LORD and do good;
dwell in the land and enjoy safe pasture . . .
But the meek will inherit the land
and enjoy great peace (Ps. 37:1–4,11).

Time Moves On

Susanne closed the door for the final time after giving yet another interview. She had decided, with her organization, that while the press offered a great opportunity to share the message of Christ with the world, they were also draining and demanding. Susanne needed to remember her needs as well as her children's. With an audible sigh of relief she reached for the chain on the door and pulled it across. Her body was weary. The last nine weeks had taken their toll.

Susanne headed for the living room, picking up a pot of chai on the way. The sun was almost below the horizon, casting long shadows into the room. Pulling back the net curtain, she opened the door, allowing the cool evening breeze to enter.

With the children playing outside she began to pray.

Life would go on for Susanne. It had to. This wasn't the end. Tilmann's life was gone and he had been called home to glory, but Susanne's call to serve her Master remained.

'I'm not the super-holy type people think I am,' said Susanne, attempting to convince us that her actions were how every Christian would react. 'Before the Lord we are all the same, everyone has their own work to do.' Susanne knew her role and ministry had just become that much harder, but remained convinced she was doing what the Lord was asking of her. She continued to stress she was not superior just because she worked miles from her homeland.

'We happen to be here in Turkey but actually we live the same life as we did in Germany and in England. I have a family, I have to wash up, I have to look after my kids, and I have neighbours to look after, just like everyone else back home. The only thing is I have to learn a new culture and language. All the other jobs are daily chores that you do wherever you are in the world. Just living and having to take your body with you but as you do it, doing it for the glory of God and the spread of His great news!'

Despite her resolute attitude to stay in Malatya and her wholehearted passion for sharing the gospel, Susanne knows not to expect easy times ahead. As the whirlwind and bubble of the media attention moved on to the next big story, it began to dawn on Susanne just how tough it would be. It didn't change the reason she was in Turkey though. For years now she had loved and yearned for the Turkish people. Now among them, she was not going to let anything steal her away, even the tragic murder of her husband.

'It would be very easy for me to get angry about Turkey and the people here but I don't want to make difficulties. I want to try to forgive, like Jesus forgave me. I want them to hear the news of Jesus. I want to tell them that all the strength they have seen in me is not from me; it's just from the Lord and the fact that people prayed for me.'

Reminding herself of her commitment to Christ, Susanne pulled out her pretty memories box from under the desk in the study. Taking off the lid, she delved about for a moment before bringing out a diary. 'Ah ha,'

Susanne declared triumphantly, obviously pleased she had found the item in her hand. She flicked back and forth through a few pages, before settling on one and saying, 'Here we are . . .'

> *Our Father in heaven I ask not for being healthy or ill, for life or for death, I just ask that you watch over my being healthy or being ill, alive or dead for Your glory and my salvation. You only know what is good for me; you are my only Lord do what you want. Give to me, take from me but make your will my will.*

It was her diary entry from the Friday evening of 20 January 1989. Smiling knowingly as she read to the end of her prayer from that night, Susanne paused. Was that commitment and desire still the same today?

'This is what I always wanted – to make His will my will. Sometimes I don't know what to do, to go this way or that way. But my wish was always that God's will would be my will in all situations all through my life. "Do whatever you want," I was saying, "but may I always do what You want."'

Afterword

As we tap away at our computers, in the safety of my office, we are preoccupied with the remarkable woman we met just a few months ago. We're piecing together these final words of what has been an emotional, real life journey and we cannot, we must not forget those final moments we spent with the most remarkable of women, and two of her three delightful children. Before the hotel concierge whistled loudly across the forecourt, waking the taxi driver from his nap, we had something to ask Susanne. We just couldn't return home without discovering the answer.

'Why?' Why had she allowed two young people into her home and into her life, at a time of deep vulnerability and even greater emotion? We had been asking her intruding and personal questions about her life and, more crucially, details of the death of her beloved husband. She could have so easily ignored our emails and phone calls during any period of this project, closing the door in our face, leaving her story untold. Was it fame? This lady had endured the world's media on her doorstep for weeks – she didn't need fame. Was it money? Susanne asked nothing about the financial ramifications of her story being sold across the world. So what was it?

No, Susanne knew why she was allowing us to pry and probe into her life, and almost before the word 'why' had left my lips, she was telling us.

'In my life as a Christian, both here in Turkey and back home in Germany, I have witnessed too many "submarine Christians", Christians who on Sundays pop their head up above the "water", make an appearance, but for Monday through to Saturday spend their week submerged. Christians are no longer standing out from the crowd; no longer are people daring to be different. Too many are hiding themselves away 'til Sunday comes, when they suddenly come back to life. I hope that the story of my husband, and his two friends' outright commitment to Christ might challenge today's church to no longer hide under the "water", but that they might rise, be strong and declare the mighty name of Jesus across the world.'

'Then Jesus said to his disciples, "If anyone would come after me, he must deny himself and take up his cross and follow me. For whoever wants to save his life will lose it, but whoever loses his life for me will find it."'

'The future: yes I worry about it, but I try not to think about it. I realize that I have a big responsibility with my kids, to try to bring them up. I also have the church here, and that is partly my responsibility, but am I alone? No! I'm not by myself. I have a great family, plus my organization and my colleagues. Most of all I have my God. I am not alone.'

We were left in awe of this courageous woman of God. Here she was, a grieving widow carrying her cross, dying daily to herself, despite the cries of grief and tremendous pressures all around beckoning her to give up.

There is an old hymn that Jonathan's mother used to sing to him: Susanne fulfils it.

❋　　　❋　　　❋　　　❋

Dare to be a Daniel.
Dare to stand alone!
Dare to have a purpose firm!
Dare to make it known.[27]

To the glory of God and in loving memory of three of His children who died as martyrs for Him

Ugur Yüksel 1975 – 2007
Necati Aydin 1972 – 2007
Tilmann Geske 1961 – 2007

'Precious in the sight of the Lᴏʀᴅ
is the death of his saints'
(Ps. 116:15).

Bibliography

Busch, W., *Jesus: Our Destiny* (Arlington, USA: Collection IPS, 1993).

dc Talk, *Live Like a Jesus Freak: Spend today as if it were your last* (Minnesota, USA: Bethany House Publishers, 2001).

Marsh, C., *Too Hard for God?* (Milton Keynes: Authentic Lifestyle, 2000).

Peretti, F., *Present Darkness: a novel* (Chicago, USA: Tyndale House, 2003).

Endnotes

1 FEG stands for Freie Evangelische Gemeinde – a German association of free evangelical churches encompassing both the charismatic and the conservative.

2 A *chador* is a traditional garment: a black, full-length semi-circle of fabric open down the front. It is thrown over the head and held shut at the front.

3 The Alpha course was devised by Nicky Gumbel at Holy Trinity Brompton, London.

4 Adapted from notes on http://www.thenagain.info/WebChron/Mediterranean/Nero.html (accessed 15 August 2007).

5 Modern Language Association (MLA): "Martyrdom." WorldNet 3.0. Princeton University.<www.Dictionary.com http://dictionary.reference.com/browse/Martyrdom> (accessed 15 August 2007).

6 See 1 Peter 3:15.

7 Isaiah 53:2–9, The Message.

8 Susanne has asked us not to recount details of the torture.

9 On the day of the murder, Tilmann's body had been identified by a member of their company. What he saw matched the coroner's report.

10 cf. Joshua 1:5.

11 Ephesians 3:20.

12 cf. 1 Peter 3:15.

[13] Matthew Henry (Eighteenth-century commentator).

[14] Romans 8:19.

[15] Romans 8:38.

[16] cf. Revelation 21:5.

[17] cf. John 14:1–4.

[18] 'Father God, I Wonder,' by Ian Smale. Copyright © Ian Smale Kingsway's Thankyou Music.

[19] Author unknown.

[20] Excerpts from 'Blessed be Your Name' by Beth and Matt Redman. Copyright 2002 Thankyou Music. Used with permission.

[21] cf. 2 Corinthians 12:9.

[22] 'How Can I Keep from Singing? © 2006 Alletrop Music/BMI (admin. by Music Services)/Worshiptogether.com Songs/Sixsteps Music ASCAP/Thankyou Music (admin. by EMI Christian Music Publishing). All Rights Reserved. Used by Permission.

[23] http://news.bbc.co.uk/1/hi/world/europe/4688518.stm and http://en.wikipedia.org/wiki/Andrea-Santoro (accessed 6 August 2007).

[24] www.opendoors.org.uk (accessed 10 July 2007).

[25] Quoted by E. Lyle in 'Wasted Lives?', Open Doors *Frontline* magazine (June 2007).

[26] At the time of writing Susanne has not yet been able to visit the men in prison; she is attempting to make this happen.

[27] Written by Philip P. Bliss in 1873.